Engaging Writing Activities

Engaging Writing Activities

Objective-Driven Timed Exercises for Classroom and Independent Practice

Michelle Lindsey and Heather Garcia

ROWMAN & LITTLEFIELD
Lanham • Boulder • New York • London

Published by Rowman & Littlefield
An imprint of The Rowman & Littlefield Publishing Group, Inc.
4501 Forbes Boulevard, Suite 200, Lanham, Maryland 20706
www.rowman.com

86-90 Paul Street, London EC2A 4NE

Copyright © 2024 by Heather Garcia and Michelle Lindsey

All rights reserved. No part of this book may be reproduced in any form or by any electronic or mechanical means, including information storage and retrieval systems, without written permission from the publisher, except by a reviewer who may quote passages in a review.

British Library Cataloguing in Publication Information Available

Library of Congress Cataloging-in-Publication Data

Names: Lindsey, Michelle, author. | Garcia, Heather, author.
Title: Engaging writing activities : objective-driven timed exercises for classroom and independent practice / Michelle Lindsey and Heather Garcia.
Description: Lanham, Maryland : Rowman & Littlefield Publishing Group, 2024.
Identifiers: LCCN 2023041183 (print) | LCCN 2023041184 (ebook) |
  ISBN 9781475869309 (cloth) | ISBN 9781475869316 (paperback) |
  ISBN 9781475869323 (ebook)
Subjects: LCSH: English language—Composition and exercises—Study and teaching (Secondary)—Activity programs. | Composition (Language arts)—Study and teaching (Secondary)—Activity programs.
Classification: LCC LB1631 .L439 2024 (print) | LCC LB1631 (ebook) |
  DDC 808/.0420712—dc23/eng/20230913
LC record available at https://lccn.loc.gov/2023041183
LC ebook record available at https://lccn.loc.gov/2023041184

Contents

Preface		xiii
Introduction		xv

Section One: 5-Minute Exercises — 1

Exercise	Objective	3
1	Identify and Emulate Tone	3
2	Write with Detail	3
3	Evaluate Plot	4
4	Analyze Diction	4
5	Use Source Material to Stem Poetry	5
6	Write with Imagery and Vivid Verbs	5
7	Incorporate Details into Writing	6
8	Outline Sonnets	6
9	Create Themes	7
10	Write with Immediacy	7
11	Enhance Emotion Using Polysyndeton	8
12	Create Mystery	8
13	Examine Tone and Characterization	9
14	Write with Creative Diction and Attention to Detail	9

15	Write Descriptively Using Tone and Purpose	10
16	Rewrite Cliches	10
17	Brainstorm Plotlines	11
18	Use Syntax to Create Drama	11
19	Practice Writing Byronic Heroes	12
20	Identify and Emulate Tone	13
21	Revise for Specific Details	14
22	Incorporate Antithesis	14
23	Practice with Setting	15
24	Write with Imagery	15
25	Practice with Argumentation	16
26	Incorporate Personification	16
27	Practice with Oxymorons	17
28	Use Conflict to Drive Plot	17
29	Practice Incorporating Tone	18
30	Use Evidence to Build Arguments	18
31	Write to a Specific Audience	19
32	Write to Respond to Quotes	19
33	Create Tone in Writing	20
34	Write with Careful Selection of Detail	20
35	Practice with Setting	21
36	Plan a Podcast	21
37	Practice with Connotation and Denotation	22
38	Practice with Elaboration	22
39	Evaluate Arguments	23
40	Practice with Characterization	23
41	Adjust Pacing Using Polysyndeton	24
42	Evoke Rich Tone through Dialogue	24

43	Practice with Themes in Nonfiction Writing	25
44	Create Strong Characterization	25
45	Write Character Dialogue and Body Language	26
46	Practice with Argumentation	26
47	Utilize Plotlines to Develop a Theme	27
48	Examine Tone and Characterization	28
49	Revise for Stronger Verbs	28
50	Analyze Characterization	29
51	Write Argumentatively	29
52	Analyze Metaphors	30
53	Utilize Plotlines to Develop a Theme	31
54	Incorporate Anaphora	32
55	Write About Setting	32
56	Write Conflicted Characters	33
57	Introduce a Theme Using Dialogue	33
58	Write with Imagery and Action	34
59	Evaluate Themes	34
60	Create a Scene Using Source Material	35
61	Enhance Writing with Asyndeton	36
62	Analyze Diction and Its Effects	37
63	Practice with Rhetoric in Argumentative Writing	37
64	Examine Tone and Characterization	38
65	Practice Writing Horror	38
66	Practice with Argumentation and Connotation	39
67	Use Stems to Draft Microfiction	39
68	Create Scenarios to Teach Lessons	40
69	Practice with Rhetoric in Argumentative Writing	40
70	Write a Dream Sequence while Practicing with Perspective	41

71	Write to Match Tone	42
72	Write Using the Senses	43
73	Write Descriptions	43
74	Write in the First-Person Point of View	44
75	Write a Poem with Focus on Syllables	44
76	Write Concisely	45
77	Practice with Argumentation	45
78	Write Using Showing, Not Telling	46
79	Use Stems to Draft Microfiction	46
80	Map Out Fictional Worlds	47
81	Practice with Point of View	47
82	Use Sentence Stems as Inspiration	48
83	Write Using Vivid Verbs	48
84	Recreate a Story from a Different Perspective	49
85	Brainstorm Novel Ideas Using Fears	49
86	Practice Creating Characterization	50
87	Write Argumentation with Descriptive Detail	50
88	Use Source Material to Stem Writing	51
89	Analyze Metaphors	52
90	Develop Characterization	52
91	Write with En Dashes	53
92	Write with Imagery	53
93	Emulate Literary Elements	54
94	Create a Character	55
95	Use Synonyms to Express Intensity	56
96	Respond to Quotes	56
97	Practice with Bildungsroman	57
98	Create an Image Using Vivid Imagery	57
99	Analyze Similes	58

100	Continue a Story by Matching Tone	58
101	Write with Evocative Adjectives	59
102	Enhance Writing by Incorporating Interjections	59
103	Write Dynamically to Increase Audience's Interest	60
104	Create Symbolism	61
105	Analyze Language	61
106	Practice with Character Archetypes	62
107	Write to Respond to Quotes	62
108	Write with Vivid Verbs	63
109	Explore Plot	63
110	Create a Scene	64
111	Write Using Rich Details and Imagery	65
112	Evoke a Certain Tone and Practice with Plot	65
113	Write Intentionally	66
114	Defend a Stance with Specific Details	66
115	Explore Symbolism	67
116	Practice Writing Hyperbole	67
117	Write Convincingly	68
118	Create Meaningful Plotlines	68
119	Write for a Specific Audience	69
120	Write with En Dashes	69
121	Write with Specific Details	70
122	Practice with Setting Archetypes	70
123	Write to Describe an Object	71
124	Rearrange Plot Points to Create a Dynamic Story	71
125	Write to Incorporate Specific Details	72
126	Write with En Dashes	72
127	Write with Synonyms to Create Mood	73
128	Revise for Specific Details	73

| 129 | Practice with a Communion Scene | 74 |
| 130 | Create Arguments Using Rhetoric | 74 |

Section Two: 25-Minute Exercises — 75

Exercise	Objective	77
131	Write Vividly Using Strategically Selected Details	77
132	Write Descriptively Using Imagery	78
133	Create a Character	79
134	Develop an Extended Metaphor	80
135	Rewrite Using Adjectives	81
136	Create Immersive Settings and Recreate Historical Places	82
137	Create a Character While Reworking Archetypes	83
138	Write with Believable Dialogue	84
139	Develop an Argument Supported by Textual Evidence	85
140	Revise Sentences to Add Sensory Detail	86
141	Practice Creating Immersive Settings	87
142	Create Tone in Writing	88
143	Create a Backstory Incorporating Vivid Details	89
144	Develop an Argument Supported by Textual Evidence While Analyzing Tone	90
145	Practice Writing Dialogue and Showing vs. Telling	92
146	Create a Journal or Diary Entry Rich in Imagery	93
147	Incorporate Details and Diction to Enhance Tone	95
148	Practice with Characterization and Drama	96
149	Practice with Genres and Plot	97
150	Use Sentences from Previously Published Works to Create New Scenes	98
151	Practice with Indirect Characterization and Drama	99
152	Create Imagery that Appeals to All Five Senses	100

153	Write Flash Fiction	101
154	Enhance Sentences with Strategic Verb Choices and Tense Shifts	102
155	Enhance Descriptive Writing by Selecting Specific Details	103
156	Create Symbols	104
157	Write Dynamically to Increase Audience Interest	105
158	Write Poetry	106
159	Practice with Characterization and Tone	107
160	Practice with Different Genres of Writing	108

Section Three: 45-Minute Exercises		**109**
Exercise	**Objective**	**111**
161	Eliminate Filler Words in Narrative Writing	111
162	Evaluate Rhetoric and Practice Using Rhetoric in Argumentation	113
163	Analyze Poetry for Important Literal and Figurative Meaning and Use that Analysis to Construct a Commemorative Poem	115
164	Create a Setting Incorporating Vivid Details and Clear Imagery	117
165	Evaluate an Opening to a Novella and Then Create an Opening to a Different Novella Modeling What was Done Well and Changing What Could be Better	118
166	Write an Epilogue while Incorporating Literary Elements	120
167	Write a Scene with Rich Action	122
168	Use Poetry to Stem Narrative Fiction While Practicing With Imagery	123
169	Analyze the Effectiveness of Dialogue and Showing vs. Telling	125
170	Redesign a Classic Scene for a Young Adult or Middle-Grade Audience	127
171	Write a Fictional Scene from Two Sources	129

172	Use Historical Documents to Stem Fiction	131
173	Analyze and Recreate an Argument	133
174	Use Poetry to Stem Narrative Fiction and Practice with Indirect Characterization	135
175	Write a Fictional Scene from Two Sources	137
176	Determine Purpose and Use Textual Evidence to Write Argumentatively	139
177	Write Scenes Based on Poetry	141
178	Practice with Setting and Imagery	142
179	Create Scenes Based on Source Material	144
180	Create Characters Based on Tone	145

| About the Authors | 147 |

Preface

This book is designed to help writers. All writers. It doesn't matter if you are a freshman in high school or a seasoned writer with dozens of published novels; we want all writers to gain skills, confidence, and inspiration by using this book (although if you have dozens of published novels and are using this book, we will absolutely swoon).

The irony is that far too many writing books can be stifling. These can be far too regimented and can strip writers of their unique voices. Many people turn to writing books to help their craft when, in reality, it might be diminishing their intuitive writing voice.

We tried really hard to avoid this.

We don't ask you to change your voice or follow a predetermined formula for success. We try to help you find, polish, and nurture your writing voice. We want to inspire your creativity, not mold it into something we think it should be. Our purpose with these exercises is to promote creative thinking and exploration in a low-stakes way.

We curated our experiences as educators and authors to create a book we wanted to have that simply didn't exist. There are numerous books for writers filled with hundreds of prompts to launch writing, but those don't always stretch writers beyond their comfort zones. This book provides multiple opportunities to enhance your craft while providing skill-targeted exercises that could launch amazing writing projects.

We hope someone, hopefully you, will turn these exercises into the next best-selling book.

Of course, as educators, our brains are hardwired to make this resource suitable to not only writers of all levels of experience but to teachers with all levels of experience too—because we are all about making the lives of teachers easier.

These exercises will help energize and engage writers who may be victims of an over-tested generation. Our goal is for students of writing (whether still in school or well-beyond school) to enjoy writing *and* enhance their craft. We need writers who are willing to think creatively, edit their work stylistically, and share their writing with the world.

Introduction

As you explore this book, you have the opportunity to make it suit your needs. Each exercise has distinct time allotments to fit within your schedule, or you can utilize the table of contents to jump to certain skills you want to enhance.

Teachers, we have created 180 exercises—which means writers can engage in an exercise every single school day without requiring you to make a single lesson plan. Each exercise has its own writing objective with easy-to-follow, step-by-step directions. But if you are not a teacher, 180 exercises is still a hearty number of concentrated writing experiences meant to enhance your writing craft and engage you in writing exercises.

SECTION ONE

Section One consists of 130 exercises that can each be completed in under five minutes!

Teachers, these exercises are perfect for bell ringers, brain breaks, or exit tickets.

- Bell Ringers: When students enter the room, have the exercise displayed on the board (or in a handout) with a five-minute timer. Bell ringers are great for getting students settled and working immediately while you take attendance, steal a sip of coffee, take calming breaths before dealing with your rowdiest class, or whatever needs to be done in those precious silent five minutes. This sends the message to students that they will be working in your class from the moment they enter the room.
- Brain Breaks: Our students have attention spans that can last for mere seconds. We can probably thank social media for that. However, teachers need

to decide if they are going to work within the constraints of these attention spans or work against them. If you want the path of least resistance, incorporate five-minute brain breaks into your lessons. If your plan for the day is attention-heavy, meaning you are lecturing, kids are note-taking or watching long videos, etc., then you might want to pause halfway through and use one of the five-minute writing exercises as a brain break. It's still academic, but it gives their brains a rest from the long lesson and allows them a chance to refocus when the five-minute writing burst ends.
- Exit Tickets: It's best practice to keep students engaged up until the very last moment of class. However, sometimes our lesson plan times are off, and we might finish a few minutes earlier than expected. When this happens, you can display one of the five-minute exercises to keep kids engaged right up to the ringing of the bell.

If you are not a teacher, section one is *still* for you. These five-minute exercises will ask you to work with sentence starters, offer "would you rather" scenarios, provide quotes for analysis, allow practice with literary devices, and stretch your revision skills and ability to write towards a specific goal. These are perfect to get your creativity flowing and can easily turn into longer projects.

SECTION TWO

Section Two consists of thirty exercises which can all be completed in under twenty-five minutes. These exercises are more in-depth than the five-minute prompts and are sometimes accompanied by source material.

In this section, we ask writers to examine novel openings, brainstorm novel ideas, work on characterization, build worlds, design settings, develop themes and tone, and engage with historical artifacts.

Transitioning from short five-minute activities to longer twenty-five-minute activities doesn't need to be a "graduation" moment. These activities aren't any more challenging than those that came previously; they just require a bit of thought and a little more time to complete well. There is no need to hold off on using this section of the book until the first section is completed.

As educators, this section might be our favorite. It allows enough time for teachers to still incorporate bell ringers, other housekeeping tasks, and opportunities for extension activities. As writers, we love this section because it is designed to offer writers strong bones for longer works. These exercises can stand alone and are still accompanied by objectives, but for those writers who are looking for larger projects, these twenty-five-minute exercises might spark something truly amazing.

SECTION THREE

Section Three consists of twenty exercises which can all be completed in under forty-five minutes. We capped the timing at forty-five minutes because that's the duration of an average class period, but if more time is needed to complete these exercises, nobody will object.

Like the other sections, Section Three has objectives for each task with clear directions that can be easily implemented in the classroom or your writing routine.

Many exercises in this section can also be turned into longer pieces, but a unique feature in Section Three is that ALL prompts have stimulus material or mentor texts to prompt the writing activities.

In secondary classrooms, many standards revolve around the implementation of source material. Not only will writers enhance their reading skills, but they will also enhance their writing skills in engaging ways. In this section, we ask writers to practice with rhetoric, imagery, epilogues, poetry, etc. We also offer the opportunity for writers to read and write across different genres.

IMPORTANT CONSIDERATIONS

We recommend keeping all writing in one location because these exercises lend themselves to being enhanced in future writing experiences. Because whether writing is done in five minutes or forty-five minutes, that is not a lot of time to create polished pieces. Through thoughtful revision, these exercises could be extended and have a lifespan beyond 180 days.

Revision includes:

- changing the order of sentences
- replacing phrases
- adding specificity to the writing
- creating new sentences where the meaning might be unclear
- cutting unnecessary sentences

Revision is an important part of the writing process and requires practice, which will hopefully happen with the writing from some of your favorite exercises.

GETTING STARTED

Regardless of your purpose for using this book, we hope you find it engaging and we hope you find inspiration within the pages. Our goal is that these exercises help you hone your craft and find a voice that makes you a unique and successful writer.

We also want to give you the opportunity to publish your work. Once you complete your favorite exercise, revise it, and make it something you're proud of, be sure to send it to us through our website so we can consider publishing it on www.teacherswithtips.com. By sending us your work, you are agreeing to its publication on our website for the world to see.

We also have another request. This one is selfish, and we own that. If you find true inspiration, meaning one of these exercises inspires your next best-selling novel, we would like an invite to your book-launch party or book-signing event so we can purchase a signed copy of YOUR book. Just sayin'.

Section One

5-Minute Exercises

EXERCISE 1

Objective: Identify and Emulate Tone

Task: Use the 1936 photo (figure 1.1) by Dorothea Lange, *Migrant Mother*, as an inspiration for your writing. Create a moment or scene within a novel that matches the tone in the photograph.

Figure 1.1 (Exercise 1) Migrant Mother. *Source*: Lange, Dorothea, photographer. Destitute pea pickers in California. Mother of seven children. Age thirty-two. Nipomo, California. United States Nipomo San Luis Obispo County California, 1936. March. Photograph. https://www.loc.gov/item/2017762891/.

EXERCISE 2

Objective: Write with Detail

Task:

Step One: List fifteen things that can break easily.

Step Two: Choose one and describe it in its broken state without naming it. Try to ensure that the reader can tell what the item once was.

EXERCISE 3

Objective: Evaluate Plot

Task:

Step One: Consider the list of plotlines provided. Rank the plotlines on a scale of one to five. One being the lowest, least interesting to you, and five being the highest, most interesting to you.

1. A love story where the couple has its troubles—but they power through.
2. A plane crash with survivors stranded on an island.
3. An action-packed race for survival that has a happy ending- but only for some people.
4. A murder mystery where everyone is a suspect.
5. A forbidden love story that ends in tragedy.

Step Two: Now, imagine all five plotlines exist within the same novel. Explain how awesome (or not) this novel would be.

EXERCISE 4

Objective: Analyze Diction

Task: The common phrase "toxic" is often used to explain a bad relationship or a person. Consider the actual meaning of "toxic." Considering what "toxic" means, what is this saying about a relationship or a person if they are compared to something toxic? Then, evaluate this insult. How harsh is it to be called this?

EXERCISE 5

Objective: Use Source Material to Stem Poetry

Task:

Step One: Don't read the following excerpt from Lewis Carroll's *Alice's Adventures in Wonderland,* published in 1865. Instead, scan the excerpt your eyes and write down the first six words your eyes land on.

> Alice was not a bit hurt, and she jumped up on to her feet in a moment: she looked up, but it was all dark overhead; before her was another long passage, and the White Rabbit was still in sight, hurrying down it. There was not a moment to be lost: away went Alice like the wind, and was just in time to hear it say, as it turned a corner, "Oh my ears and whiskers, how late it's getting!" She was close behind it when she turned the corner, but the Rabbit was no longer to be seen: she found herself in a long, low hall, which was lit up by a row of lamps hanging from the roof.

Step Two: Write a six-line poem incorporating each word into each line.

EXERCISE 6

Objective: Write with Imagery and Vivid Verbs

Task: What/who would be the scariest thing/person to have to run from? Describe this thing/person in detail using vivid imagery and verbs to describe their actions. Vivid words tend to evoke strong emotional reactions from readers or create clear images in a reader's mind.

EXERCISE 7

Objective: Incorporate Details into Writing

Task: Imagine you are asking a friend or family member to find something for you in your room. At first, keep the details vague and capture their responses. Slowly reveal more specific details as the conversation continues.

EXERCISE 8

Objective: Outline Sonnets

Task: Elizabethan sonnets typically follow the same pattern. The first quatrain (the first four lines) typically introduces a problem. This can be any problem. The second quatrain (lines 5–8) usually complicates the problem or includes the author's stake in the problem. The third quatrain (lines 11–14) usually seeks out a solution to that problem. Then, the rhyming couplet at the end usually includes some closure to the problem.

With these rules in place, plan a quick sonnet.

Quatrain 1: What problem would you introduce?
Quatrain 2: What would you say to complicate it or show your involvement with the problem?
Quatrain 3: What is needed to solve the problem? Or what is the process to discover a solution?
Rhyming Couplet: What is the closure?

EXERCISE 9

Objective: Create Themes

Task: Change is a common thematic idea present in literature. Change can be detrimental or beneficial.

Step One: List three examples of change that could be detrimental.
Step Two: List three examples of change that could be beneficial.
Step Three: List one change that could be both detrimental and beneficial at the same time.

EXERCISE 10

Objective: Write with Immediacy

Task: Write an opening sentence to a novel. The goal is to make your readers care instantly about the character. Just telling readers the character is in danger might not be enough to make readers care, because they don't know your character yet.

EXERCISE 11

Objective: Enhance Emotion Using Polysyndeton

Task: Polysyndeton is the deliberate insertion of conjunctions, and the typical effect is to slow down the sentence and compound the details. They add up. The most common conjunctions used are "and" and "or".

Imagine your character is incredibly overwhelmed with work or school. Write a scene where your character details everything on his or her to-do list. Try to use more than four conjunctions.

EXERCISE 12

Objective: Create Mystery

Task: Imagine you just bought a house, and you found an old trunk in the attic from the previous owner. What would be the most mysterious thing you would find in that trunk? Explain why it would be the most mysterious thing and what you would do once you found it.

EXERCISE 13

Objective: Examine Tone and Characterization

Task: Use the acrostic below to brainstorm a novel. The acrostic is the title of the book. First, decide on what premise would be fitting for this title and then use the letters within the title to brainstorm the details of the novel. For example, if wanting to write about a failed marriage, the "W" could say: a woman discovers an earth-shattering secret about her husband while he's away on a business trip. For "R", say: reality hits when she must decide if she wants to stay faithful to her husband and keep his secret or report it to the police.

W
R
E
C
K
E
D

EXERCISE 14

Objective: Write with Creative Diction and Attention to Detail

Task: Without using the words zoo, cages, animals, or people, describe a zoo to someone who doesn't know what one is. Pay attention to the details you include and try to incorporate creative word choices.

EXERCISE 15

Objective: Write Descriptively Using Tone and Purpose

Task: Using five of the ten words listed below (you may change the derivation to suit your needs), write a short description of a character performing a task of your choosing. Be sure to have the character depicting a desperate or frantic tone in your description.

Divert	Kick	Stumble	Eager	Begged
Sincere	Pursuit	Hasten	Cries	Attempts

EXERCISE 16

Objective: Rewrite Cliches

Task: Cliches are overused phrases writers often want to avoid.

Step One: Examine the following cliches to determine their meaning.

- Think outside the box
- Raining cats and dogs
- Loose cannon

Step Two: Rewrite those three cliches so they have more pizzazz. You can add as many words as you need to provide a more unique and dazzling sentence.

EXERCISE 17

Objective: Brainstorm Plotlines

Task:

Step One: Make a massive list of as many 100 things as you can. For example, 100 years, 100 flowers sent for a birthday, 100 candles, etc. List as many as you can in two minutes.

Step Two: Choose one that would make the best title for a novel or movie. Explain what the novel or movie might be about with your remaining time.

EXERCISE 18

Objective: Use Syntax to Create Drama

Task: Imagine you are impulsively writing your resignation letter to the worst job you've ever had. Your resignation letter will be five sentences long. However, you need to vary your sentence length to add emphasis and drama.

- Your first sentence should only be 1-3 words.
- Your second sentence should be 10-15 words.
- Your third sentence should be between 1-3 words.
- Your fourth sentence should be 10-15 words.
- Your final sentence should be 1-3 words.

EXERCISE 19

Objective: Practice Writing Byronic Heroes

Task: A Byronic hero is a character who is typically cynical, sarcastic, and might even be narcissistic and egotistical. However, at the same time, they seem to lure people in and have a way about them that people feel drawn to. They seem to struggle between doing the right thing and the wrong thing in many situations as they struggle with selfish motivations. They also tend to go against societal expectations.

Outline three scenes where these characteristics would be evident for a character.

1.

2.

3.

EXERCISE 20

Objective: Identify and Emulate Tone

Task: You will have five minutes to fabricate the scene that might have happened just before this picture was taken. The picture (figure 1.2) is titled *Bathers at Alameda* and was published by Bain News Service in 1910.

Be sure the moment matches the tone of the picture.

Figure 1.2 (Exercise 20) Bathers at Alameda. *Source*: Bain News Service, Publisher. Bathers at Alameda. California, ca. 1910. [Between and Ca. 1915] Photograph. https://www.loc.gov/item/2014694861/.

EXERCISE 21

Objective: Revise for Specific Details

Task: Rewrite the following sentences by using more precise words for the ones that are in bold. A sample has been completed for you:

Sample: The **dog ran** through the **yard**.
Revised Sample: The **golden retriever romped** through the **leaf-covered grass**.

Your sentences to revise:

- The **tree fell** on the **house**.
- The **girl went** up the **hill**.
- The **man ran** to the **store**.

EXERCISE 22

Objective: Incorporate Antithesis

Task: Antithesis is when two completely opposite things or people exist in writing. It is meant to highlight those differences. It typically follows the same grammatical structure.

Step One: Examine the sample and determine what it means.
  You're easy to lose but hard to forget.

Step Two: Create your own sentence incorporating antithesis. It might be helpful to use the words "yet" or "but."

EXERCISE 23

Objective: Practice with Setting

Task: Think about an experience you would like to have (a vacation at the beach, snow tubing, etc). Then, fill in the chart below by listing all the things you could see, hear, taste, smell, etc. Be as specific in your list as possible. You can use this list to add detail to future writing.

Experience:

What do you see?	What do you hear?	What do you taste?	What do you smell?	What do you feel?

EXERCISE 24

Objective: Write with Imagery

Task:

Step One: If you could master any hobby or skill, what would it be? Write one sentence describing that hobby.

Step Two: In a sentence rich with imagery, describe what mastery of that hobby or skill would actually look like for you.

EXERCISE 25

Objective: Practice with Argumentation

Task: Imagine you are writing a novel from the perspective of a war journalist who accidentally travels back in time. Which war do you think would make the best setting for a novel? Be sure to defend your answer.

- Revolutionary war
- Civil War
- World War I
- World War II
- Vietnam

EXERCISE 26

Objective: Incorporate Personification

Task: Write a breakup letter to something nonliving that probably shouldn't be in your life as much as it is. For example, you could break up with coffee, shopping, a holiday, etc. Treat the nonliving object of your letter as if it's a living breathing entity. Be sure to detail why you are breaking up with this *thing* in the letter.

For example, if breaking up with coffee, you could write "you're bad for my health" or "I can't sleep because of you."

EXERCISE 27

Objective: Practice with Oxymorons

Task:

Step One: Explain the following oxymorons.
What does it mean if someone is

1. Perfectly imperfect
2. Defiantly submissive
3. Willfully ignorant

Step Two: Write your own. Think of an adjective to describe someone you know. Then, pair that adjective with its antonym but in a way that makes sense.

EXERCISE 28

Objective: Use Conflict to Drive Plot

Task:

Step One: Imagine you are on a trip with a large group of people. List eight things that could be catastrophic if they occurred on this trip.

Step Two: Choose three out of the eight things you listed, and explain how effective these plot points would be in creating conflict within a story.

EXERCISE 29

Objective: Practice Incorporating Tone

Task: Write a scene where a character goes through the emotional range provided. They should start angry and get progressively angrier. Be sure to *show* these emotions and not tell them.

Emotional Range: displeased to irritated to furious to hostile

---

EXERCISE 30

Objective: Use Evidence to Build Arguments

Task: Consider the following scene from Emily Bronte's *Wuthering Heights,* published in 1847. In this scene, Heathcliff admits to digging up his beloved's grave.

Step One: Read the scene.

> I'll tell you what I did yesterday! I got the sexton, who was digging Linton's grave, to remove the earth off her coffin lid, and I opened it. I thought, once, I would have stayed there: when I saw her face again—it is hers yet!—he had hard work to stir me; but he said it would change if the air blew on it, and so I struck one side of the coffin loose, and covered it up: not Linton's side, damn him! I wish he'd been soldered in lead. And I bribed the sexton to pull it away when I'm laid there, and slide mine out too; I'll have it made so: and then by the time Linton gets to us he'll not know which is which!

Step Two: Explain if this is an incredibly romantic or creepy gesture. Be sure to defend your argument using evidence from the excerpt.

EXERCISE 31

Objective: Write to a Specific Audience

Task:

Step One: Brainstorm a speech about a social issue for a specific audience.

What audience would you choose to target? _____

What does this group of people believe? _____

What does this group of people value? _____

What might make them angry? _____

Step Two: Write an opening line of your speech that will either infuriate this audience or delight them.

EXERCISE 32

Objective: Write to Respond to Quotes

Task:

Step One: Read the following sentiment from the Greek Philosopher, Plato: "People are like dirt. They can either nourish you and help you grow as a person, or they can stunt your growth and make you wilt and die."

Step Two: Who in your life serves as nourishing soil? Make a list of these people and then choose one to write a few sentences about.

EXERCISE 33

Objective: Create Tone in Writing

Task:

Step One: Read the opening line from Edgar Allan Poe's "The Fall of the House of Usher," written in 1839. While you read, circle or list all the words that create an ominous or melancholic tone.

> DURING the whole of a dull, dark, and soundless day in the autumn of the year, when the clouds hung oppressively low in the heavens, I had been passing alone, on horseback, through a singularly dreary tract of country, and at length found myself, as the shades of the evening drew on, within view of the melancholy House of Usher.

Step Two: Rewrite the sentence by changing all the words that you circled or listed into words that have a more joyous or whimsical tone. What is the effect?

EXERCISE 34

Objective: Write with Careful Selection of Detail

Task: What is one item that you own or a skill you possess that you would want to hand down to the next generation? Describe that object or skill using precisely selected details without actually saying what the object or skill is.

EXERCISE 35

Objective: Practice with Setting

Task:

Step One: Imagine what the world will be like in 200 years. Describe it. Be sure to discuss specific details.
What do these look like:

- Cars
- Jobs
- Politics
- Schools
- Clothing
- Social media
- Houses

Step Two: Now, explain why this would make a good setting for a novel.

EXERCISE 36

Objective: Plan a Podcast

Task: Plan a five-episode podcast series.

Step One: Decide what topic you would want to cover.
Step Two: Explain what your episodes or topics would be.
Step Three: Give your podcast an amazing, catchy title.

EXERCISE 37

Objective: Practice with Connotation and Denotation

Task:

Step One: Consider the word "magic" and its many meanings, associations, and contexts.

   List as many different meanings and contexts as you can. Try to get at least five.

Step Two: Choose two out of the five and create a premise for a novel that would incorporate both meanings or contexts.

EXERCISE 38

Objective: Practice with Elaboration

Task: Would you rather someone pay to send you on an amazing, month-long trip to a foreign country, OR, would you rather someone buy you a brand-new car and a year's worth of gas?

Explain the benefits of your choice and focus on elaborating. Whenever you think you are done writing, ask yourself, "but why," and keep writing.

EXERCISE 39

Objective: Evaluate Arguments

Task: Evaluate Senator Barack Obama's sentiment toward the people of Chicago on February 5, 2008, before winning his first presidential election.

> Change will not come if we wait for some other person or if we wait for some other time. We are the ones we've been waiting for. We are the change that we seek.
>
> Barack Obama (2008)

Step One: To what extent do you think this quote helped persuade voters to lean toward him?

Step Two: Would this quote have the same effect on today's audience? Explain your answer.

EXERCISE 40

Objective: Practice with Characterization

Task: Imagine you are writing a very petty and dramatic character. Your character just found out their friend sabotaged their chances of getting a date with someone they were interested in.

What is your character's revenge?

EXERCISE 41

Objective: Adjust Pacing Using Polysyndeton

Task: Polysyndeton is a writing tool that allows readers to slow down and focus on the words in the sentence with a renewed weight because conjunctions are used close together without punctuation.

Step One: Read the following sentence:

> He feared her for her loud voice and her wild hair and her wicked smile and her unconquerable spirit.

Notice when you read that each element he feared gets its own spotlight.

Step Two: Now, list four things you like (or dislike) about a person and finish the following sentence using polysyndeton:

> I was drawn to/away from _____ because of their _____ and _____ etc.

EXERCISE 42

Objective: Evoke Rich Tone through Dialogue

Task: Use dialogue between two or more characters to reveal someone coming unhinged. Meaning, someone is on the verge of losing either their temper or their mind. Every line should be dialogue. Instead of saying "says", try to use something that will show the unhinging instead of saying it. Things to say besides "says": utters, remarks, alleges, whispers, snarls, spouts, asserts, murmurs, gasps, etc.

EXERCISE 43

Objective: Practice with Themes in Nonfiction Writing

Task: Imagine you won an award for something you created. It will be expected that at the award ceremony, you will need to deliver a speech. Consider the following themes listed below. Choose three you think would belong in the best acceptance speech. Be sure to explain why.

Fear of failure	Power	Sacrifice	Hope	Empowerment
Fulfillment	Celebration	Future	Knowledge	Patience

EXERCISE 44

Objective: Create Strong Characterization

Task: Use the opening line provided to finish the scene below. It can go in any direction you want but you need to characterize your narrator as fierce and bold. Do this in a way that shows the characteristics, do not just say them. Think about what a fierce person looks, acts, and thinks like, and emulate that in the scene.

Your opening: The door slams behind me as I step out onto the crowded sidewalk. Eyes closed, breathing deeply, I give myself a moment. My eyes open slowly and adjust to the blaring sun and that's when I see it.

EXERCISE 45

Objective: Write Character Dialogue and Body Language

Task:

Step One: Read the following stanza taken from Emily Bronte's poem written in 1837 titled "Last Lines."

> Though earth and moon were gone,
> And suns and universe ceased to be,
> And thou were left alone,
> Every Existence would exist in thee.

Step Two: Create a scene where one character has given this stanza to another character. How would the receiver react? What would he or she say? What would his or her body language be?

EXERCISE 46

Objective: Practice with Argumentation

Task: Argue which setting would be best for a horror novel. Be sure to explain your answer thoroughly.

Option One: Dense, untraveled woods
Option Two: Isolated private island with a mansion on it
Option Three: An old burned-down building teenagers use as a party spot

EXERCISE 47

Objective: Utilize Plotlines to Develop a Theme

Task:

Step One: Pair up the provided thematic ideas with the plotlines listed below.

Themes:

- Manipulation
- Desire to escape
- Facing Darkness

Plotlines:

- Someone receives a mysterious threat of blackmail.
- One person wakes up and doesn't remember who they are and is covered in dirt and blood.
- People try to convince a character he's crazy—but he doesn't feel crazy. He thinks they are the crazy ones.

Step Two: Choose one pair and explain how you would develop that plotline in order to develop that thematic idea. There are no wrong answers.

EXERCISE 48

Objective: Examine Tone and Characterization

Task: Use the acrostic below to explain what a character would need to be doing or thinking to evoke the tone provided. Use each letter of the tone word to reveal what would need to happen within a scene to create the tone: Hostile. For example, "H" could be hurling a chair.

H
O
S
T
I
L
E

EXERCISE 49

Objective: Revise for Stronger Verbs

Task: Spend three minutes writing about your morning. Include as many details about your morning as you can in the three minutes. Next, circle or list every verb and replace at least five of them with more precise verbs. See below for an example:

Original Sentence: I woke up at 6:00 am when my alarm rang.
Revised Sentence: I reluctantly rose from my bed at 6:00 am when my alarm chimed, breaking through the silence of the room.

EXERCISE 50

Objective: Analyze Characterization

Task: Below are the opening lines to a scene. You need to finish the scene. It can go in any direction you want but you need to characterize your narrator as timid and insecure. Do this in a way that shows the characteristics, do not just say them. Think about what a timid and insecure person looks, acts, and thinks like, and emulate that in the scene.
Your opening:

> This interview could change my life. If only I could muster enough control to slow my racing heart.
> "Reagan Evans?" a woman asks while peeking her head around a heavy oak door, "they're ready for you now."

EXERCISE 51

Objective: Write Argumentatively

Task: Imagine poems that explore the struggles of lost love. This love could be all different types of love. Based on the titles below, decide which type of lost love would be discussed in each poem. Defend your ideas.

Option One: "The Dark River"
Option Two: "Untethered"

EXERCISE 52

Objective: Analyze Metaphors

Task:

Step One: Analyze the metaphor delivered by Abraham Lincoln in his *House Divided* Speech given in Springfield, Illinois in 1858. Explain what it means.

> A house divided against itself cannot stand.
>
> - Abraham Lincoln

Step Two: Analyze the metaphor written by William Shakespeare in *As You Like It*, Act 2, Scene 7. Explain what it means.

> All the world's a stage, and all the men and women merely players. They have their exits and their entrances.
>
> - William Shakespeare

Step Three: Which metaphor is stronger? Explain.

EXERCISE 53

Objective: Utilize Plotlines to Develop a Theme

Task:

Step One: Pair up the provided thematic ideas with the Plotlines listed below.

Themes:

- Family
- Survival
- Justice

Plotlines:

- Someone is convicted of a crime they didn't commit, and they know someone on the jury.
- Two people searching for survivors of a plane crash on their own because search and rescue won't do it.
- Someone objecting at a wedding when asked if anyone has an objection to the bride and groom getting married.

Step Two: Choose one pair and explain how you would develop that plotline to highlight that thematic idea. There are no wrong answers.

EXERCISE 54

Objective: Incorporate Anaphora

Task: Write a quick note to your friend who happens to be in jail with you. It has to be fast because you are slipping the note into his or her hand as the guard escorts you to your cell. Begin your note with anaphora. Meaning, you should repeat a word or phrase at the beginning of two or more sentences.

EXERCISE 55

Objective: Write About Setting

Task: If you were forced to move to a brand-new city, what criteria would this city need to have for you to be excited about moving there?

Step One: Brainstorm specific landmarks, restaurants, stores, entertainment venues, parks, housing, etc. that would make this area appealing.

Step Two: Write the opening of a scene where a young person is describing the town's features to a parent who lives far away.

EXERCISE 56

Objective: Write Conflicted Characters

Task: In cartoons, we often see a character's struggle between a right or wrong choice represented by an angel on one shoulder and a devil on the other.

Write a scene where your character is emulating this type of moment. You don't necessarily need to include the angel and devil, but it should be very clear your character is having a moral dilemma.

EXERCISE 57

Objective: Introduce a Theme Using Dialogue

Task: Consider the two different types of survival listed below. Then, create a moment of dialogue between two fictional characters. The relationship between the characters is up to you. It can be between a boss and employee, parent and child, customer and employee, etc. In your dialogue, try to introduce the two thematic ideas without saying them.

The thematic ideas: physical survival and emotional survival

EXERCISE 58

Objective: Write with Imagery and Action

Task:

Step One: Set a timer for two minutes and in those two minutes, list as many red things as you can.

Step Two: From your list of red items, circle or list four.

Step Three: Write a sentence that includes each of these four items and ensure your sentence has lively action as well as imagery. You may not use the word "red" in your sentence.

EXERCISE 59

Objective: Evaluate Themes

Task: Consider the list of twelve themes below. Group the themes into four categories, each category can only have three themes. When you group them, explain which themes would coexist together within one novel.

injustice	greed	rebellion	coming of age
chaos	capitalism	facing darkness	free will
isolation	society	fear of failure	gender roles

EXERCISE 60

Objective: Create a Scene Using Source Material

Task: This photograph (figure 1.3) is from the Library of Congress, and it was taken in 1905 and is titled, *Miss Clara Blackburne and Sonnette II (Maltese Terrier)*.

Try to imagine who took this photo back in 1905.

- Who is behind the camera?
- What is this person's life like?
- How is he or she connected to the woman in the photograph?
- What was the interaction like right before this picture was taken?
- What is Miss Blackburne looking at off in the distance?
- What happened right after this picture was taken?

Jot down as many notes about this interaction as you can.

Figure 1.3 (Exercise 60) Miss Clara Blackburne. *Source*: Bain News Service, Publisher. Miss Clara Blackburne and "Sonnette II" Maltese Terrier. Photograph. Retrieved from the Library of Congress, <www.loc.gov/item/2014683012/>.

EXERCISE 61

Objective: Enhance Writing with Asyndeton

Task: When a writer creates a sentence that utilizes asyndeton, it means he or she writes a sentence with a series that does NOT include conjunctions like *and*. The purpose of writing a sentence like this is that it enhances the pace of the sentence and makes it seem more important than the other sentences surrounding it.

Step One: Read this example of asyndeton from *Heart of Darkness* by Joseph Conrad, published in 1899:

> Imagine the growing regrets. The longing to escape. The powerless disgust, the surrender—the hate.

As the sentence comes to a close, the emotions get more intense.

Step Two: Write one sentence where you focus on a single emotion and follow the pattern set in the example above, where the emotion gets amplified as the sentence continues.

For example, you could write, "Imagine the increased happiness. The urge to smile. The remorseless glee, the lightness—the joy."

EXERCISE 62

Objective: Analyze Diction and Its Effects

Task: Nelson Mandela was an advocate for peace, civil rights, and emotional and physical health in South Africa. Mandela gave a speech titled "Lighting Your Way to a Better Future" at the launch of the Mindset Network, which was a group promoting health and education in this region. Read the quote, then analyze the diction.

> Education is the most powerful weapon we can use to change the world and Mindset Network is a powerful part of that world-changing arsenal.
>
> -Nelson Mandela, July 16, 2003

Step One: Explain the connotation of the words "weapon" and "arsenal".

Step Two: Explain why Mandela would use these words and what effects these choices have.

EXERCISE 63

Objective: Practice with Rhetoric in Argumentative Writing

Task: Use the emotional appeal (Pathos) to write a thirty-second to one-minute pitch convincing a bank to loan you $2,000. You only get this limited time frame to convince the bank you need it.

EXERCISE 64

Objective: Examine Tone and Characterization

Task: Use the acrostic below to explain what a character would need to be doing or thinking to evoke the tone provided. Use each letter of the tone word to reveal what would need to happen within a scene to create the tone: desperate. For example, for the letter "d", a character might be "darting her bloodshot eyes to every corner of the room scouring for a solution." Try not to use the word "desperate" in your response.

D
E
S
P
E
R
A
T
E

EXERCISE 65

Objective: Practice Writing Horror

Task: Write a two-sentence horror story using an abandoned carousel as your setting. Your horror story can *only* be two sentences.

EXERCISE 66

Objective: Practice with Argumentation and Connotation

Task: Imagine you need to convince a boss in an interview that you really need the job.
   Evaluate the three tones and decide which tone would be more convincing:

Delighted   Triumphant   Eager

Be sure to explain your answer.

EXERCISE 67

Objective: Use Stems to Draft Microfiction

Task:

Step One: Choose two of the following phrases to incorporate into a fifty-word short story. This moment will be more focused on language and characterization and not on plot considering the limited number of words.

Step Two: Once you choose two, use one as the first line of your scene and the other as the last line. You can change the tenses to match your writing.

- The rain began to fall
- That was when the accident happened
- She is lying
- He can't do that
- I didn't realize just how wrong I was
- I have to leave
- This wasn't supposed to happen like this

EXERCISE 68

Objective: Create Scenarios to Teach Lessons

Task:

Step One: Read Aesop's fable below titled "The Young Crab and His Mother," published in the 1400s.

> "Why in the world do you walk sideways like that?" said a Mother Crab to her son. "You should always walk straight forward with your toes turned out."
> "Show me how to walk, mother dear," answered the little Crab obediently, "I want to learn."
> So the old Crab tried and tried to walk straight forward. But she could walk sideways only, like her son. And when she wanted to turn her toes out she tripped and fell on her nose.
> *Do not tell others how to act unless you can set a good example.*

Step Two: Make a list of other scenarios that could teach readers the same lesson.

EXERCISE 69

Objective: Practice with Rhetoric in Argumentative Writing

Task: Use the emotional appeal (Pathos) and the logical appeal (Logos) to write a thirty-second to one-minute speech convincing a jury you are not guilty of the crime you were accused of committing. You only get this limited time frame to convince the jury you're innocent.

EXERCISE 70

Objective: Write a Dream Sequence while Practicing with Perspective

Task: The following image (figure 1.4) is called *Ascension du 26 septembre 1876, 700 mètres,* and was drawn by Albert Tissandier.

Write a dream from a character using the picture as inspiration.

You can either write from the perspective of a six-year-old or a ninety-six-year-old.

Figure 1.4 (Exercise 70) Ascension. *Source*: Tissandier, Albert, Artist. Ascension du 26 septembre, 700 mètres / Albert Tissandier. [Between 1876 and 1880] Photograph. Retrieved from the Library of Congress, <www.loc.gov/item/2002735698/>.

EXERCISE 71

Objective: Write to Match Tone

Task:

Step One: Read the poem, "Night" by Francis William Bourdillon, written in 1895.

> The night has a thousand eyes,
> And yet the day but one;
> Yet the light of the bright world dies
> With the dying sun.
>
> The mind has a thousand eyes,
> And the heart but one;
> Yet the light of a whole life dies,
> When love is done.

Step Two: Use the final line of the poem as the opening of a sentence for a free write.

Step Three: Once you get past the opening, continue writing while incorporating some of the words from the poem into your free write and try to match the tone of the poem.

EXERCISE 72

Objective: Write Using the Senses

Task:

Step One: What is your favorite comfort food? Describe how that food smells, the texture of the food, and how the food makes you feel, but do NOT describe how it tastes.

EXERCISE 73

Objective: Write Descriptions

Task:

Step One: List six things that make you smile.

1.
2.
3.
4.
5.
6.

Step Two: Choose one and write a sentence where you describe what it is and why it makes you smile.

Step Three: Revise that sentence to remove the name of the thing that you listed but try to make sure readers can still tell what the thing is.

EXERCISE 74

Objective: Write in the First-Person Point of View

Task: Imagine you are walking over a bridge at dusk and just as you reach the top of the bridge, thousands of bats come flying out from underneath the bridge to head out to forage for their nightly meal. What does this experience sound like? What does it feel like? Write about the experience in the first-person point of view using as much sensory detail as possible.

EXERCISE 75

Objective: Write a Poem with Focus on Syllables

Task:

Step One: Read the following poem written in 1851 by Lord Alfred Tennyson called "The Eagle." Notice that each line in the poem has eight syllables.

> He clasps the crag with crooked hands;
> Close to the sun in lonely lands,
> Ring'd with the azure world, he stands.
>
> The wrinkled sea beneath him crawls;
> He watches from his mountain walls,
> And like a thunderbolt he falls.

Step Two: Choose an animal to write a poem about and try to write the poem so that each line has the exact same number of syllables.

EXERCISE 76

Objective: Write Concisely

Task:

Step One: Write about a hobby or skill you want to learn. Write for three minutes without stopping.

Step Two: Review your writing and remove 5–10 words to create more concise writing. You might need to rearrange some words to create complete sentences once the 5–10 words are removed. (Hint, the word "that" can usually be removed without needing to make any revisions.)

EXERCISE 77

Objective: Practice with Argumentation

Task: Consider the "would you rather" scenario detailed below. Choose which one you would rather do and write a convincing argument defending why it's the better option.

Would you rather

* Present on stage to hundreds of people on a topic you don't know anything about

or
* Prepare for weeks on a flawless presentation that you are passionate about only to present to an empty audience because no one chose to come?

EXERCISE 78

Objective: Write Using Showing, Not Telling

Task: Write a paragraph describing a goal you have obtained and explain the feeling you experienced upon obtaining that goal. The only rule is that you must SHOW your emotions, not TELL us what your emotions were.

EXERCISE 79

Objective: Use Stems to Draft Microfiction

Task:

Step One: Choose two of the following phrases that capture your attention to incorporate into a fifty word short story. This moment will be more focused on language and characterization and not on plot considering the limited number of words.

- The secret would be too heavy to keep
- I can't do this anymore
- I don't recognize that person anymore
- I can't choose, don't make me choose
- The wind howled, sounding like a pack of wolves on the hunt
- The snow would soon cover the roof of the house

Step Two: Use one line you chose as the first line to your story and the other as the last line.

EXERCISE 80

Objective: Map Out Fictional Worlds

Task: If you owned and lived in an apartment building with fifteen units and got to fill it with ONLY your favorite people, who would you put in the units closest to yours, who would you put in the units farthest from you, and who wouldn't get a spot in the apartment building at all?

Step One: Draw a map of the apartment building and add names of where everyone would be placed.

Step Two: Write a few sentences explaining why they are placed where they are.

EXERCISE 81

Objective: Practice with Point of View

Task: Choosing the right point of view to depict a scenario is crucial. Imagine a five-year-old character watching fireworks for the first time.

Step One: Write a sentence in the third person recapping his experience.
Step Two: Now rewrite that experience but in the first person. Remember, you would be five. You will need to change some details.
Step Three: Explain which version you like better.

EXERCISE 82

Objective: Use Sentence Stems as Inspiration

Task:

Step One: Read the following quote from the book *The Art of Living: The Classical Manual on Virtue* by Epictetus, a Greek Stoic Philosopher.

> Don't just say you have <u>read books</u>. Show that through them you have learned to <u>think better</u>, to be a more <u>discriminating</u> and <u>reflective</u> person. <u>Books</u> are the training weights of the <u>mind</u>. They are very helpful, but it would be a bad mistake to suppose that one has made progress simply by having <u>internalized</u> their <u>contents</u>.

Step Two: Remove all the underlined words and replace them with your own words to create a new, wise saying about a topic of your choosing such as hockey, running, or baking. Be sure to match the parts of speech for the words you are replacing.

EXERCISE 83

Objective: Write Using Vivid Verbs

Task: What is one thing you have difficulty doing consistently? Describe this activity using the most vivid verbs possible. Avoid lackluster verbs in your writing (such as clean) and instead choose more specific verbs that create a clearer image of the task (such as polish, rinse, or scour).

EXERCISE 84

Objective: Recreate a Story from a Different Perspective

Task:

Step One: Read Aesop's fable, written in the 1400s, below, titled "The Crow and the Pitcher."

> In a spell of dry weather, when the Birds could find very little to drink, a thirsty Crow found a pitcher with a little water in it. But the pitcher was high and had a narrow neck, and no matter how he tried, the Crow could not reach the water. The poor thing felt as if he must die of thirst.
> Then an idea came to him. Picking up some small pebbles, he dropped them into the pitcher one by one. With each pebble the water rose a little higher until at last it was near enough so he could drink.
> *In a pinch a good use of our wits may help us out.*

Step Two: Retell this story from the point of view of an older person watching the crow.

EXERCISE 85

Objective: Brainstorm Novel Ideas Using Fears

Task:

Step One: List five things you're afraid of.

Step Two: Imagine a novel where a character had to overcome one of those fears. Which fear would make the most exciting novel? Explain.

EXERCISE 86

Objective: Practice Creating Characterization

Task:

Step One: Read the opening of the 1910 poem "The Fascination of What's Difficult" by William Butler Yeats.

> The fascination of what's difficult
> Has dried the sap out of my veins, and rent
> Spontaneous joy and natural content
> Out of my heart.

Step Two: Describe a character who might carry the opening of this poem around in their pocket. What does this person look like? What is their occupation? Who do they spend time with? Describe this person using rich imagery. Include details that are unique to this person.

EXERCISE 87

Objective: Write Argumentation with Descriptive Detail

Task: Imagine that a multimillion-dollar hotel is being built in your community. There is space for twenty-five shops at the bottom level of this hotel and you have just been given the opportunity to open a business in one of the shop locations. What business would you open? Describe it in detail and explain why you think this business would thrive in the hotel environment.

EXERCISE 88

Objective: Use Source Material to Stem Writing

Task:

Step One: Look at the image (figure 1.5) taken by M. H. Zahner in 1900 from the Library of Congress, which depicts the aftermath of a major hurricane in Galveston, Texas.

Figure 1.5 (Exercise 88) Aftermath of Hurricane. *Source*: Zahner, M. H. Galveston Disaster, Trying to Find Where Their Home Stood. Niagara Falls, N.Y: M. H. Zahner, publisher. Photograph. Retrieved from the Library of Congress, <www.loc.gov/item/98503906/>.

Step Two: Use the picture to brainstorm ideas for two completely different novels.

EXERCISE 89

Objective: Analyze Metaphors

Task:

Step One: List five actions that are dangerous. This can be skydiving without an instructor, sticking a fork in an outlet, swimming with sharks, etc.

Step Two: Choose one of the dangerous actions from your list. Compare falling in love to that dangerous action using a metaphor. Use the stem for help:

Falling in love with him/her is [insert dangerous action].

Step Three: Explain the meaning of that metaphor in the context of falling in love.

EXERCISE 90

Objective: Develop Characterization

Task: Write a scene with two people walking along the beach at midnight. What are they saying to one another? What is their body language like? What can we learn about them from the way they interact with each other? Use characterization to create realistic characters in this specific setting.

EXERCISE 91

Objective: Write with En Dashes

Task:

Step One: Write two sentences about something that brings you joy.

Step Two: Combine those two sentences into one single sentence using an en dash (–) to create emphasis. See the sample below:

> Original Sample: Being outside brings me joy. But I do not prefer being bitten by mosquitoes.
>
> Revised Sample: Being outside brings me joy – but not during mosquito season.

Step Three: Continue writing on this topic incorporating en dashes when appropriate.

EXERCISE 92

Objective: Write with Imagery

Task: Describe a hippopotamus to a person who has never seen one. Use as many of the five senses as you can.

EXERCISE 93

Objective: Emulate Literary Elements

Task:

Step One: Read the following sentence from Bram Stoker's 1897 classic, *Dracula*. As you read the sentence below, you may want to consider Stoker's use of alliteration, imagery, and personification as examples of literary elements to emulate.

> To add to the difficulties and dangers of the time, masses of sea-fog came drifting inland-white, wet clouds, which swept by in ghostly fashion, so dank and damp and cold that it needed but little effort of imagination to think that the spirits of those lost at sea were touching their living brethren with the clammy hands of death, and many a one shuddered as the wreaths of sea-mist swept by.

Step Two: Choose one example of a literary element to emulate in a sentence of your own. Your sentence can be about anything you wish, but if you need an idea, you could write about a weather event as Stoker did.

5-Minute Exercises 55

EXERCISE 94

Objective: Create a Character

Task: This photograph (figure 1.6) is from the Library of Congress, and it was taken by Samuel Herman in 1919 of a little girl named Doris Gottscho holding a fish. Try to imagine who took this photo back in 1919, jot down as many ideas as you can.

- Who is behind the camera?
- What is this person's life like?
- How is he or she connected to the child in the photograph?
- What was the interaction like right before this picture was taken?
- What about right after?

Figure 1.6 (Exercise 94) Dorris Gottscho. *Source*: Gottscho, Samuel H, photographer. Reference prints, -1920, numbers 2133 to 2377. Doris Gottscho, holding fish and fishing pole, sitting on a fence III. Photographed 1919 or 1920. Photograph. Retrieved from the Library of Congress, <www.loc.gov/item/2018751046/>.

EXERCISE 95

Objective: Use Synonyms to Express Intensity

Task:

Step One: Create a continuum of words that are synonyms, but that increase in intensity. See the sample below:

⟶

content   pleased   happy   delighted   exuberant

Step Two: Now, practice creating your own continuum on the lines below:

⟶

sad   despondent

⟶

damaged   irreparable

EXERCISE 96

Objective: Respond to Quotes

Task: After reading the following quote from Ralph Waldo Emerson, an American poet and transcendental writer in the 1800s, explain what Emerson is trying to say about the role books play in his life. Why might he have chosen food to make this comparison?

> I cannot remember the books I've read any more than the meals I have eaten; even so, they have made me.

EXERCISE 97

Objective: Practice with Bildungsroman

Task: A bildungsroman is a coming-of-age story. It's when a character has some sort of realization or awakening. Usually, the character develops either morally or psychologically. Imagine a bildungsroman novel that weaves in a theme of the desire to escape. What could three plotlines look like?

EXERCISE 98

Objective: Create an Image Using Vivid Imagery

Task:

Step One: Read the following excerpt from *The Haunted and the Haunters* by Sir Edward Bulwer-Lytton, published in 1859.

> In one of the drawers we found a miniature portrait set in gold, and retaining the freshness of its colors most remarkably, considering the length of time it had probably been there. The portrait was that of a man who might be somewhat advanced in middle life, perhaps forty-seven or forty-eight. It was a most peculiar face- a most impressive face.

Step Two: Write a few sentences explaining what you think the face in the portrait may have looked like. Use vivid imagery in your description.

EXERCISE 99

Objective: Analyze Similes

Task:

Step One: List five things that can be messy at any point. This can be a mirror that breaks, a dog rolling in mud, etc.

Step Two: Choose one of the messy things from your list. Compare a breakup to that messy thing using a simile.

Step Three: Explain the meaning of that simile in the context of the breakup.

EXERCISE 100

Objective: Continue a Story by Matching Tone

Task:

Step One: Read the following sentence from *Irish Fairy Tales* Edited by W.B. Yeats in 1892.

> It was a wild, blowing night; never in all my born days did I see such a night—the darkest night that ever came out of the heavens. I did not know where I was for the life of me.

Step Two: Use this sentence to start a piece of writing of your own. Who is out on this night? Where is he or she going? Is someone expecting them? Be sure to match the tone of this opening.

EXERCISE 101

Objective: Write with Evocative Adjectives

Task:

Step One: Finish the sentence below with one word.

"I cannot imagine a more perfect _____."

Step Two: Continue writing to describe what makes it perfect using the most evocative adjectives possible. Evocative adjectives should capture the emotion of readers or create clear images in a reader's mind.

EXERCISE 102

Objective: Enhance Writing by Incorporating Interjections

Task:

Step One: Read the following sentence from Wilkie Collins' short story, "The Fatal Fortune," published in 1874, and notice how the dashes are used to interrupt the sentence, to interject additional or clarifying information.

> My dear father - though I was far from deserving his kindness—entered into the matter heart and soul.

Step Two: Using the sentence above as a model, write two sentences about people you know that include dashes that separate clarifying information.

EXERCISE 103

Objective: Write Dynamically to Increase Audience's Interest

Task: Use the following image (figure 1.7), titled *Prison, Ekaterinburg,* as inspiration and write a movie or novel pitch that sells this movie or novel. The image was initially published by Bain News Service and depicts women standing outside a Russian prison in 1919 with food for their imprisoned relatives.

Your pitch should include:

- What the main action or conflict is (without spoilers)
- An introduction to a relatable character the audience can care about
- Rich vocabulary and adjectives to describe the plot

Your movie or novel pitch should be about seventy words.

Figure 1.7 (Exercise 103) Prison Ekaterinburg. *Source*: Bain News Service, Publisher. Prison, Ekaterinburg. Photograph. Retrieved from the Library of Congress, <www.loc.gov/item/2014708679/>.

EXERCISE 104

Objective: Create Symbolism

Task:

Step One: Read the following line from Nathaniel Hawthorne's 1850 novel, *The Scarlet Letter* where Hawthorne uses a black flower to symbolize fate.

> It is our fate. Let the black flower blossom as it may.

Step Two: Make a list of five to seven other physical objects that could symbolize fate.

Step Three: Then, recreate Hawthorne's sentences using one of YOUR objects.

EXERCISE 105

Objective: Analyze Language

Task:

Step One: Read the following sentence from Mary Shelley's classic novel *Frankenstein,* published in 1818, when Monster tells Dr. Frankenstein:

> Beware; for I am fearless, and therefore powerful.

Step Two: Think about that phrase and, in a few sentences, reflect on what that line truly means. What is meant by the word "powerful"? How is one "fearless"?

EXERCISE 106

Objective: Practice with Character Archetypes

Task:

Step One: Choose two of the following archetypes from the list below.

the lover	the magician	the outlaw	the sage
the explorer	the innocent	the jester	the everyman

Step Two: Make them best friends. Create a scene in a novel where their archetypical nature shines. Be sure to detail the action and utilize dialogue to make those characteristics stand out.

EXERCISE 107

Objective: Write to Respond to Quotes

Task: The Ancient Greek philosopher, Plato, once said, "There are two things a person should never be angry at: What they can help, and what they cannot."

Step One: Make a list of five to ten things that make you angry.

Step Two: Cross out each item on your list that is something you can help or something you cannot help and examine what is left on your original list. Write a few sentences explaining what you think Plato was trying to tell people with this quotation.

EXERCISE 108

Objective: Write with Vivid Verbs

Task:

Step One: Read the following sentence from Bram Stoker's 1897 classic, *Dracula*, and circle or list the verbs used.

> Then came another rush of sea-fog, greater than any hitherto—a mass of dank mist, which seemed to close on all things like a grey pall, and left available to men only the organ of hearing, for the roar of the tempest, and the crash of the thunder, and the booming of the mighty billows came through the damp oblivion even louder than before.

Step Two: Write a sentence using the verbs *close, roar, crash,* and *booming,* without writing about a storm.

EXERCISE 109

Objective: Explore Plot

Task: Imagine you have been put in charge of managing a failing independently owned bookstore. Your job is to make certain that it makes a profit and that it benefits the community. How would you save this bookstore? Make a list of all the things that could happen that could save this bookstore from financial ruin.

EXERCISE 110

Objective: Create a Scene

Task: This photograph (figure 1.8) from the Library of Congress was taken sometime between 1870 and 1890 and it is titled, *Bill Drennan, Indian scout and companion of Kit Carson / N. H. Rose, San Antonio, Texas, photographer.*

Try to imagine who took this photo back in the late 1800s.

- Who is behind the camera?
- Why would this person be taking a photo of Bill Drennan?
- How is the photographer connected to Bill?
- What was the interaction like right before this picture was taken?
- What happened right after this picture was taken?

Jot down as many notes about this interaction as you can.

Figure 1.8 (Exercise 110) Bill Drennan. *Source*: Library of Congress: Bill Drennan, Indian scout and companion of Kit Carson / N. H. Rose, San Antonio, Texas, photographer. 1870-1890. https://www.loc.gov/pictures/item/94505022/.

EXERCISE 111

Objective: Write Using Rich Details and Imagery

Task: Many people of influence use what is called a capsule wardrobe where they intentionally limit themselves to a few pieces of clothing they wear over and over again in different ways, or they have a signature style because it saves them time getting ready in the morning. If this was something you were forced to do, what would be in your capsule wardrobe? Describe five pieces of clothing in rich detail using imagery that appeals to both visual and tactile senses. (What do the clothes look like? How do the textures feel?)

EXERCISE 112

Objective: Evoke a Certain Tone and Practice with Plot

Task: In Medias Res, the beginning of a story takes place right in the middle of a major drama or conflict in a novel.

Step One: Choose one of the following tones you would want to evoke in an opening.

   Tone 1: Turmoil
   Tone 2: Regret

Step Two: Write an opening scene that evokes that specific tone and captures the essence of In Medias Res.

EXERCISE 113

Objective: Write Intentionally

Task: When the title of a novel appears in the text, it is typically a very important moment.

Step One: Imagine a novel about a nineteen-year-old girl moving to New York to pursue her dreams of modeling. However, in the process of auditioning, struggling to find work, and battling with her self-image, she meets someone who makes her realize modeling might not be what she wants for her future.

The title of the novel is *As Dawn Approaches.*

Step Two: Write a scene in this novel that incorporates the title in a meaningful way. The title will only appear once, so make it count.

EXERCISE 114

Objective: Defend a Stance with Specific Details

Task: If there was one chore that you could make someone else do for the rest of your life, what would that chore be, who would you have complete this task for you, and why? Be as specific in your explanation as possible.

EXERCISE 115

Objective: Explore Symbolism

Task: Symbolism is a concept where a physical object represents some other concept. For example, an owl symbolizes wisdom and intelligence.

Keeping the concept of symbolism in mind, if you had the talent to carve any animal out of wood and you could give it to someone special to you, what animal would you carve to represent this person, why would you choose that specific animal, who would you give it to, and why?

EXERCISE 116

Objective: Practice Writing Hyperbole

Task: Read the five sentences below and rewrite them using hyperbole, or exaggeration.

> Sample: The groceries are heavy.
> Revised Sample: The mountain of groceries weighs a ton.

Sentences to Revise:

- That is a big dog.
- She rode her bike fast.
- He slowly walked in.
- The rainbow was pretty.
- The tile was slick.

EXERCISE 117

Objective: Write Convincingly

Task: Would you rather own a condo on the beach or a cabin in the mountains? Explain your rationale and convince an audience that your choice is the right choice.

EXERCISE 118

Objective: Create Meaningful Plotlines

Task: Imagine the ending of a novel is:

> It was a lie. It was all a lie, and I couldn't do anything about it.

Explain what you think the novel would be about.

- How did it start?
- What was the main conflict?
- What got the characters to this point?

EXERCISE 119

Objective: Write for a Specific Audience

Task: If you were asked by your county commissioners to put a park anywhere in your county, where would you put it, what features would it include, and who would benefit from it? Write a list of ideas to submit to the county commissioners for final approval.

EXERCISE 120

Objective: Write with En Dashes

Task:

Step One: Write two sentences about a promise you would like to make to yourself or someone else.

Step Two: Combine those two sentences into one single sentence using an en dash (–) to create emphasis. See the sample below:

> Original Sample: I promise to let you play in the rain more often. But it isn't safe if there is lightning.

> Revised Sample: I promise to let you play in the rain more often – as long as there isn't lightning.

Step Three: Create two additional sentence sets using en dashes.

EXERCISE 121

Objective: Write with Specific Details

Task: Imagine you have one week with no commitments, and you have a brand-new car and unlimited gas. Where would you go, what would you do, who would you bring, and why? Use specific details in your response, so rather than say, for example, you would drive to a beach, say you would drive to sunny Southwest Florida to Siesta Key Beach in the middle of May while the sun beats on your shoulders and warms your skin.

EXERCISE 122

Objective: Practice with Setting Archetypes

Task:

Step One: Consider the following setting archetypes:

- River—usually represents a journey or a new path in life
- Maze—usually represents a dilemma or major conflict
- Tree—usually represents knowledge or growth
- Mountains— usually represent personal achievements or hardships

The list goes on to include bridges, castles, taverns, cities, etc. There doesn't seem to be a known archetypal association for a school, even though schools are depicted in all sorts of movies and novels.

Step Two: What could schools represent in literature or film? Explain your rationale.

EXERCISE 123

Objective: Write to Describe an Object

Task: You find a locked safe in the middle of the woods buried under a pile of logs and leaves. You and your best friend manage to get it unlocked. You gasp at what you see. What was hidden in this safe in the woods? Write using imagery and specific details.

EXERCISE 124

Objective: Rearrange Plot Points to Create a Dynamic Story

Task: Consider all plot points listed below. Reorder these plot points to make the most dynamic story possible. Think about which event should come first, next, after that, and then last. Order them in a way that would make a storyline no one could walk away from.

1. Experiencing a massive breakup
2. Getting promoted in a job
3. Getting fired from a job
4. Discovering a secret
5. Getting mugged
6. Losing a wallet
7. Creating something dangerous
8. Getting arrested

EXERCISE 125

Objective: Write to Incorporate Specific Details

Task: Write about a place you haven't been to in a long time. Try to remember as many details about this place as you can. What did it look like, smell like, feel like? Why did you go there? Why haven't you been back? Try to capture a feeling about the place by selecting specific details to include in your writing.

EXERCISE 126

Objective: Write with En Dashes

Task:

Step One: Write two sentences about a goal that you have for yourself.

Step Two: Combine those two sentences into one single sentence using an en dash (–) to create emphasis. See the sample below:

> Original Sample: My goal is to spend more time being in the moment. To do this I need to spend less time on my phone.
>
> Revised Sample: My goal is to spend more time being in the moment – and less time on my phone.

Step Three: Continue writing on this topic incorporating en dashes when appropriate.

5-Minute Exercises

EXERCISE 127

Objective: Write with Synonyms to Create Mood

Task:

Step One: Make a list of ten synonyms for the word "running."

Step Two: Choose one synonym that creates a sense of urgency and try to create one descriptive sentence that leaves the reader with an extreme sense of urgency.

EXERCISE 128

Objective: Revise for Specific Details

Task: Rewrite the following sentences by using more precise words for the ones that are in bold. A sample has been completed for you:

Sample: The **grasshopper jumped** through the **grass**.
Revised Sample: The **brown-speckled grasshopper leaped** through the **pristine garden scouring for a snack.**

Your sentences to revise:

- A **dog left** the **yard**.
- The **principal went** to the **office**.
- **People entered** the **mall**.

EXERCISE 129

Objective: Practice with a Communion Scene

Task:

Step One: Consider either your family or social circle. Outline the dynamic of that group. Meaning, who takes on the motherly role, who is the one-upper, who is the one who is always late, who is the most talkative, etc.?

Step Two: Write a quick scene where you all are sharing a meal. Use setting, tone, dialogue, etc. to show your readers this dynamic. Teach us about the dynamic of this group without telling us. Show us.

EXERCISE 130

Objective: Create Arguments Using Rhetoric

Task: Imagine you were accused of stealing *this* book from a store.

Use Ethos, Pathos, and Logos, to convince law enforcement you are innocent.

- Ethos: Convince them you are credible, and they should believe you
- Logos: Appeal to their logic
- Pathos: Appeal to their emotions

Section Two

25-Minute Exercises

EXERCISE 131

Objective: Write Vividly Using Strategically Selected Details

Task: Believably writing about natural disasters requires, among other writing tools, a strategic selection of details.

Step One: Make a list of five natural disasters.

1.
2.
3.
4.
5.

Step Two: Choose one that you want to work with for the rest of the exercise. Circle it on your list.

Step Three: List as many details as possible about this particular natural disaster as it is happening—the more specific the better. For example, if using a hurricane, be sure to mention the cracking of the trees as the upper limbs rip away; the crashing of debris as it smashes against the side of the house, and the howl of the wind as it tears through the attic. Notice the use of vivid verbs as well as sights and sounds. The details are specific rather than saying it is windy.

Step Four: Write a scene detailing this natural disaster including as many descriptions as you can from your list above.

EXERCISE 132

Objective: Write Descriptively Using Imagery

Task:

Step One: Recall a memory you have of a time spent in a restaurant. If you can't summon one, create a fictional one.

Step Two: For each of the five senses, brainstorm what imagery you could incorporate.

Sight: What do the walls, table settings, wait staff, floor tiles, patrons around you, etc. all look like?
Sound: What noises do the dishes on the tray make? Or what sound does the chair sliding out from under the table make, or the handling of the menu or drinkware?
Touch: What does the texture of the table feel like? The menu? The air?
Smell: What aromas surround you? Can you smell coffee? Cleaner?
Taste: What did you order? What can you taste on that first bite?

Step Three: Considering the imagery you planned, write a scene that recreates this memory. Try to incorporate as many, if not all, of the five senses in your writing. Fully immerse your reader into this moment. Make this moment sound special.

EXERCISE 133

Objective: Create a Character

Task:

Step One: Read the opening to Nathaniel Hawthorne's short story "Ethan Brand," first published in 1848.

> Bartram the lime-burner, a rough, heavy-looking man, begrimed with charcoal, sat watching his kiln, at nightfall, while his little son played at building houses with the scattered fragments of marble, when, on the hillside below them, they heard a roar of laughter, not mirthful, but slow, and even solemn, like a wind shaking the boughs of the forest.
> "Father, what is that?" asked the little boy, leaving his play, and pressing betwixt his father's knees.
> "O, some drunken man, I suppose," answered the lime-burner; "some merry fellow from the bar-room in the village, who dared not laugh loud enough within doors lest he should blow the roof of the house off. So here he is, shaking his jolly sides at the foot of Graylock."

Step Two: Now, look at this story opening from the perspective of the laughing man. What is he laughing at? What emotion is he feeling? Why is he laughing here, outside of the cottage on the hill? Does the little boy have reason to be fearful? Write this exact scene but from the perspective of the laughing man. Be sure to match the narrative structure of the original and write in the third-person past tense.

EXERCISE 134

Objective: Develop an Extended Metaphor

Task: Extended metaphors are metaphors that extend beyond the initial comparison. Elements of what is being compared continue to be included using imagery, careful diction, etc.

Step One: Begin by choosing a scenario from the following options.

- Breaking up with a significant other
- Getting fired
- Getting married

Step Two: Then, choose what you want to include within your extended metaphor.

- Train
- Ocean
- Hurricane

Step Three: Write a scene blending your selected scenario with the extended metaphor you chose. You could consider beginning by making a general comparison to the object in your metaphor. Or you can start with something completely different such as dialogue. As the scene continues to unfold, weave in other references to that metaphor to extend the metaphor.

EXERCISE 135

Objective: Rewrite Using Adjectives

Task:

Step One: Read the sentence below noting the use of adjectives. Are these adjectives helpful in visualizing the room?

> Nothing had been left undone in the furnishing of the elegant house in which she lived; rich draperies adorned the walls, tapestry of the rarest quality fittingly relieved the handsome oriental rugs and handsomely frescoed ceilings.
>
> > from "The Life Story of Southern Widow" written anonymously and published in the collection *Twenty Tales by Twenty Women: Real Life in Chicago* in 1903

Step Two: Now read a pared-down version of the sentence above, noting how all the adjectives are removed. What does the removal of the adjectives do for the sentence?

> Nothing had been left undone in the furnishing of the house in which she lived; draperies adorned the walls, tapestry relieved the rugs and ceilings.

Step Three: Using this pared-down version of the sentence as a frame, rewrite the sentence but add in adjectives of your own so we can visualize what this room looks like. You can make the room look however you see fit. You could turn the "house" in the sentence into a castle or a cabin, it is up to you, just use the sentence above as your frame.

Step Four: Insert the sentence you just created into a larger piece of writing.

EXERCISE 136

Objective: Create Immersive Settings and Recreate Historical Places

Task: Imagine you are writing historical fiction. Choose a moment in time you would want to place your setting. Strong worlds are immersive, problematic, dangerous, and written with conviction to make them believable, even if the entire world is long lost to the past.

When and where does this setting take place?	What is the weather like considering geography and season?	What does the natural background of this setting look like? Is it luscious and green, red dirt and barren (as examples)?
What is the political climate of this world?	How easily can characters navigate and move freely within this world?	How does the world as we know it change in this past setting?

EXERCISE 137

Objective: Create a Character While Reworking Archetypes

Task: Archetypes are literary forms of stereotypes. Popular archetypes include the old wise wizard, the sidekick, and the damsel in distress.

Step One: In the space below, list the characteristics of an archetypal villain and an archetypal hero.

Villain   Hero

Step Two: Create a second list where you describe a villain who does NOT meet the archetype you listed above. What characteristics might this non-archetypal villain have? Also, think of a character who might be a hero who does NOT meet the archetype listed above. Create a list below with your new characteristics.

Villain   Hero

Step Three: Write a quick scene, focusing on the non-archetypal characters, where the hero confronts the villain in a way that highlights at least one specific characteristic of both the villain and the hero.

EXERCISE 138

Objective: Write with Believable Dialogue

Task:

Step One: Imagine being forced to attend an event you did NOT want to attend. Make a list of at least ten events that you would have to be FORCED to attend.

1.
2.
3.
4.
5.
6.
7.
8.
9.
10.

Step Two: Choose one from your list above that might make an interesting setting for a confrontation.

Step Three: Think about who might have forced you to attend the event you chose from the list above. Consider the following questions: What is it about this person that made you feel compelled to attend this dreaded event? Why did you agree to attend? How did you feel while you were there?

Step Four: Write a short scene in which you confront the person who forced you to attend this event. What would you say to him or her? How might this interaction play out in a public space? Focus on your use of dialogue and keeping it authentic to the emotions of the scene.

EXERCISE 139

Objective: Develop an Argument Supported by Textual Evidence

Task: You will be given two opening scenes, both published in 1847, from two sister authors. Your task is to read the two openings and argue which opening is stronger. Be sure to cite from the excerpts to defend your stance.

Excerpt One: Wuthering Heights- *Emily Bronte*

1801—I have just returned from a visit to my landlord—the solitary neighbour that I shall be troubled with. This is certainly a beautiful country! In all England, I do not believe that I could have fixed on a situation so completely removed from the stir of society. A perfect misanthropist's heaven; and Mr. Heathcliff and I are such a suitable pair to divide the desolation between us. A capital fellow! He little imagined how my heart warmed towards him when I beheld his black eyes withdraw so suspiciously under their brows, as I rode up, and when his fingers sheltered themselves, with a jealous resolution, still further in his waistcoat, as I announced my name.
"Mr. Heathcliff!" I said.
A nod was the answer.

Excerpt Two: Jane Eyre- *Charlotte Bronte*

I was glad of it: I never liked long walks, especially on chilly afternoons: dreadful to me was the coming home in the raw twilight, with nipped fingers and toes, and a heart saddened by the chidings of Bessie, the nurse, and humbled by the consciousness of my physical inferiority to Eliza, John, and Georgiana Reed.
The said Eliza, John, and Georgiana were now clustered round their mama in the drawing-room: she lay reclined on a sofa by the fireside, and with her darlings about her (for the time neither quarrelling nor crying) looked perfectly happy. Me, she had dispensed from joining the group; saying, "She regretted to be under the necessity of keeping me at a distance; but that until she heard from Bessie, and could discover by her own observation, that I was endeavouring in good earnest to acquire a more sociable and childlike disposition, a more attractive and sprightly manner—something lighter, franker, more natural, as it were—she really must exclude me from privileges intended only for contented, happy, little children."
"What does Bessie say I have done?" I asked.
Jane, I don't like cavillers or questioners; besides, there is something truly forbidding in a child taking up her elders in that manner. Be seated somewhere; and until you can speak pleasantly, remain silent.

EXERCISE 140

Objective: Revise Sentences to Add Sensory Detail

Task:

Step One: Read through each of the unrelated sentences below. Locate the bolded noun and choose one of the five senses to use to enhance each sentence.

1. The **lawnmower** was broken.
2. **Books** were piled in a corner.
3. **Postcards** sat on a spinner rack.
4. He ate the **cookies**.
5. The sky was filled with **kites**.
6. **Dishes** sat in the sink.

Step Two: Revise each sentence to add detail to the noun and to enliven the sentence.

Sample Sentence: The **house** was new.

Sample Revision: The newest house on the block exuded fumes of fresh suburban-grey paint and too much carpet glue, and yet all the neighbors lined up at the Open House to see what details this new house had that theirs lacked, their desperation stinking up the entryway.

EXERCISE 141

Objective: Practice Creating Immersive Settings

Task: Create a futuristic world using the chart below. Strong worlds are immersive, problematic, dangerous, and written with conviction to make them believable, even if the entire world is unrealistic.

What is the weather like in this futuristic world?	How far in the future does this world take place?	What does the natural background of this world look like? Is it luscious and green, red dirt and barren (as examples)?
What is the political climate of this world?	How easily can characters navigate and move freely within this world?	How does the world as we know it change in this new world?

EXERCISE 142

Objective: Create Tone in Writing

Task:

Step One: Read the opening lines from Guy de Maupassant's short story "The Piece of String," written in 1884. As you read, circle or list all the words that capture the tone of oppression and impoverishment.

> On all the roads about Goderville the peasants and their wives were coming toward the town, for it was market day. The men walked at an easy gait, the whole body thrown forward with every movement of their long, crooked legs, misshapen by hard work, by the bearing down on the plough which at the same time causes the left shoulder to rise and the figure to slant; by the mowing of the grain, which makes one hold his knees apart in order to obtain a firm footing; by all the slow and laborious tasks of the fields. Their starched blue blouses, glossy as if varnished, adorned at the neck and wrists with a bit of white stitchwork, puffed out about their bony chests like balloons on the point of taking flight, from which protrude a head, two arms, and two feet.

Step Two: Rewrite the scene to show the opulence and wealth of the people visiting the market. Focus on changing the words that you circled or listed in your first reading to achieve the desired tone.

EXERCISE 143

Objective: Create a Backstory Incorporating Vivid Details

Task:

Step One: Consider the questions below while reading the excerpt from Arthur Morrison's short story, "*A Poor Stick*," published in 1894.

> At home, things grew worse. To return at half-past five, and find the children still undressed, screaming, hungry and dirty, was a matter of habit: to get them food, to wash them, to tend the cuts and bumps sustained through the day of neglect, before lighting a fire and getting tea for himself, were matters of daily duty.

Consider the following questions regarding the excerpt:

- Who might this caretaker be?
- What is his or her occupation?
- Where does he or she live with their family?
- What does the house look like?
- Where is the children's other parent?
- Why isn't ANYONE taking care of the children during the day?
- What do the children enjoy?

Step Two: Write a backstory for this excerpt. Show all the drama leading the characters to this dismal existence. Be as descriptive in your writing as possible being sure to include vivid details, much like the original excerpt provides.

EXERCISE 144

Objective: Develop an Argument Supported by Textual Evidence While Analyzing Tone

Task: Compare the two opening scenes written by Edgar Allan Poe. Then, analyze each piece to determine which opening creates the most dramatic tone. Be sure to use evidence from both pieces to defend your argument.

Excerpt from Loss of Breath *by Edgar Allan Poe, Published in 1832*

THE MOST notorious ill-fortune must in the end yield to the untiring courage of philosophy—as the most stubborn city to the ceaseless vigilance of an enemy. Shalmanezer, as we have it in holy writings, lay three years before Samaria; yet it fell. Sardanapalus—see Diodorus—maintained himself seven in Nineveh; but to no purpose. Troy expired at the close of the second lustrum; and Azoth, as Aristaeus declares upon his honour as a gentleman, opened at last her gates to Psammetichus, after having barred them for the fifth part of a century . . . .

"Thou wretch!—thou vixen!—thou shrew!" said I to my wife on the morning after our wedding; "thou witch!—thou hag!—thou whippersnapper—thou sink of iniquity!—thou fiery-faced quintessence of all that is abominable!—thou—thou-" here standing upon tiptoe, seizing her by the throat, and placing my mouth close to her ear, I was preparing to launch forth a new and more decided epithet of opprobrium, which should not fail, if ejaculated, to convince her of her insignificance, when to my extreme horror and astonishment I discovered that I had lost my breath.

The phrases "I am out of breath," "I have lost my breath," etc., are often enough repeated in common conversation; but it had never occurred to me that the terrible accident of which I speak could bona fide and actually happen! Imagine—that is if you have a fanciful turn—imagine, I say, my wonder—my consternation—my despair!

Excerpt from The Tell-Tale Heart *by Edgar Allan Poe, Published in 1843*

TRUE!—nervous—very, very dreadfully nervous I had been and am; but why will you say that I am mad? The disease had sharpened my senses—not destroyed—not dulled them. Above all was the sense of hearing acute. I heard all things in the heaven and in the earth. I heard many things in hell. How, then, am I mad? Hearken! and observe how healthily—how calmly I can tell you the whole story.

It is impossible to say how first the idea entered my brain; but once conceived, it haunted me day and night. Object there was none. Passion there was none. I loved the old man. He had never wronged me. He had never given me insult. For his gold I had no desire. I think it was his eye! yes, it was this!

He had the eye of a vulture—a pale blue eye, with a film over it. Whenever it fell upon me, my blood ran cold; and so by degrees—very gradually—I made up my mind to take the life of the old man, and thus rid myself of the eye forever.

EXERCISE 145

Objective: Practice Writing Dialogue and Showing vs. Telling

Task:

Step One: Think of two characters that you either invent or borrow from a book or movie that you already know.

Step Two: Write a scene where those two characters talk. Remember, dialogue follows a specific pattern of writing where:

> "One character begins talking on the first line," Alex says.
> "And the next character speaks on the next line," Michael responds.

What you have the characters saying should *not* be as mundane as the example above. You should use the dialogue to reveal a long-held secret one of the characters has been harboring. It may take multiple rounds of dialogue to reveal the whole secret.

Step Three: Once you have completed writing your big-secret reveal, rewrite that scene, but without dialogue. SHOW readers the secret. Show readers a *different* way that the other character finds out about the secret. This version should be full of action words and descriptions. This is called *showing* whereas revealing the secret was first done through *telling*.

Step Four: Which version of the big reveal are you most proud of? Which version is more engaging? Which version allows the readers to have the most emotional investment?

EXERCISE 146

Objective: Create a Journal or Diary Entry Rich in Imagery

Task: Circuses have captured the attention of audiences for over one hundred years with their splendor and larger-than-life shows and feats.

Step One: Spend some time studying the 1911 advertisement (figure 2.1) in *The Allentown Leader* for the Barnum and Bailey Circus.

Figure 2.1 (Exercise 146) The Allentown Leader. *Source*: 1911 advertisement in The Allentown Leader for the Barnum and Bailey Circus https://commons.wikimedia.org/wiki/File:1911_-_Barnum_%26_Bailey_Circus_Newspaper_Ad.jpg.

Step Two: Write a diary entry, either as someone attending the circus for the first time OR as someone who works IN the circus. Describe at least three of the acts listed in this newspaper advertisement and be sure to use striking imagery as you write. Ensure that your writing explores sensory detail in the journal or diary entry. There is no need to create a story with conflict and resolution for this. Focus on creating rich imagery.

EXERCISE 147

Objective: Incorporate Details and Diction to Enhance Tone

Task: Tone can be portrayed through:

- Word choice
- Imagery and the descriptors used
- Syntax
- Characterization—how the character perceives, handles, and reacts to whatever detail they are facing.

Step One: Write a 150–300 word opening to a novel that encompasses a dreadful tone. Use the checklist above to help you evoke the dreadful tone.

Step Two: Go back into your opening and circle or list the details you included that helped develop that dreadful tone.

Step Three: Rewrite your opening scene but change the details you circled or listed. Change the dreadful tone to a hopeful one. Use the checklist above to help you evoke a hopeful tone.

EXERCISE 148

Objective: Practice with Characterization and Drama

Task: Create a dramatic opening for a novel. The novel can be about anything. There are two rules:

- The first rule is that you must open with two staccato sentences. A staccato sentence is a one to three-word sentence that may or may not be grammatically correct but will help add drama. A few examples could look like "She fell. Fell hard." or "It happened. It finally happened." Really, they can be anything.
- The second rule is that you must encompass the following characterization within the PAIRS acronym. PAIRS is a way to analyze characterization. The "P" stands for physical description, the "A" stands for action, the "I" stands for inner thoughts, the "R" stands for reactions, and the "S" stands for speech.

P: Your character is tall, taller than six feet. Your character also has a heightened sense or ability: sight, smell, hearing, strength, etc—this is your choice. This character also has hair that reaches the bottom of their back, but they keep it loosely tied with a strip of fabric.

A: Your character is calculating, smooth with their movements, and has reflexes that seem inhuman. They are careful to keep their next move hidden.

I: Your character is rushed out of fear for someone's safety. This fear doesn't have to be for their safety though. There's a fatalistic doom pressing down on them.

R: Your character is reacting selfishly due to the worse-case-scenario thoughts racing through their mind.

S: Your character is the silent type. They choose their words carefully.

Remember, characterization is meant to be shown and not told. Your opening scene should be about 400–600 words. You can start anywhere in the plot, but you must start with two staccato sentences.

EXERCISE 149

Objective: Practice with Genres and Plot

Task: Write three different book descriptions for the following title. Each opening is for a different genre of novel. You will need to consider the words within the title and how they might shape meaning in a plot line. Consider connotation, tone, and potential themes. You might want to read the back covers of your favorite novels before you begin this exercise.

Remember, good book descriptions convince readers to read the book. In your description, you should consider including:

- A hint at the main conflict without giving away any juicy details
- Enough context to the plot so people know what it's about and can choose if it's what they're looking for, but not so much context that it spoils anything
- Strong, carefully selected diction that is enticing, rich, and provocative
- A brief introduction to the major key players and their roles within the conflict but without revealing anything crucial

Title: All Because of Lightning

Horror/thriller: Use the title to create a premise for a horror or thriller novel. Write the description that would live on the back cover.
Romance: Use the title to create a premise for a romance novel. Write the description that would live on the back cover.
Fantasy or Science Fiction: Use the title to create a premise for a fantasy or science fiction novel. Write the description that would live on the back cover.

EXERCISE 150

Objective: Use Sentences from Previously Published Works to Create New Scenes

Task:

Step One: Read the eight sentences below that come from various published works.

- "But as I walked down the steps I saw that the evening was not quite over."—*The Great Gatsby* by F. Scott Fitzgerald, published in 1925.
- "He seemed studying the familiar landscape with a stranger's and an artist's interest."—*Wuthering Heights* by Emily Bronte published in 1847.
- "The morning after I saw this apparition I was in a state of terror, and could not bear to be left alone, daylight though it was, for a moment."—*Carmilla* by Joseph Sheridan Le Fanu published in 1872.
- "The sun was coming in at the window warm and bright; the orchard on the slope below the house was in a bridal flush of pinky-white bloom, hummed over by a myriad of bees."—*Anne of Green Gables* by L. M. Montgomery published in 1908.
- "And as he walked he saw from afar men and women leaving their fields and their vineyards and hastening towards the city gates."—*The Prophet* by Kahlil Gibran published in 1923.
- "The steps drew swiftly nearer, and swelled out suddenly louder as they turned the end of the street."—*The Strange Case of Dr Jekyll and Mr Hyde* by Robert Louis Stevenson published in 1886.
- "Whilst I live on here there is but one thing to hope for, that I may not go mad, if, indeed, I be not mad already." -*Dracula* by Bram Stoker published in 1897.
- "This argument was irresistible."—*Sense and Sensibility* by Jane Austen published in 1811.

Step Two: Write a scene from a short story or a longer work where you incorporate at least four of the sentences above. Try to keep the sentences as close to their original forms as possible, but you can change tenses and points of view if needed. You can incorporate the sentences into the narration or into dialogue—whatever works best with your created scene. You will need to add a considerable amount of your own writing to connect these random sentences. As you write, consider the setting of your scene, who is in the scene, and what the conflict will be.

EXERCISE 151

Objective: Practice with Indirect Characterization and Drama

Task: Create a dramatic opening for a novel. The novel can be about anything. There are two rules.

- The first rule is that you must use the first-person point of view. Make sure we see the world through the eyes of your character.
- The second rule is that you must plan and utilize the PAIRS acronym to create indirect characterization. The "P" stands for physical description, the "A" stands for action, the "I" stands for inner thoughts, the "R" stands for reactions, and the "S" stands for speech.

Step One: Plan your character using the PAIRS acronym.

P:

A:

I:

R:

S:

Step Two: Write your opening. Remember, characterization is meant to be shown and not told. Your opening scene should be about 400–500 words. You can start anywhere in the plot, but you must write this in the first-person point of view and you must use indirect characterization.

EXERCISE 152

Objective: Create Imagery that Appeals to All Five Senses

Task: Dinner scenes are very important and difficult to write. How the dinner unfolds reveals a lot about the relationships between the characters involved. How people behave, react, feel, think, etc. all provide implications for their interpersonal dynamics.

Your task is to write a failed dinner scene. This dinner needs to be so catastrophically bad that there is no denying the tension and conflict between the characters.

Your only rule is to include all five senses. You must select how you create this imagery carefully because a harmonious dinner where ham is served shouldn't smell like roasted flesh left in the sun for weeks before being cooked. Choose your details carefully. This scent wouldn't match the vibe. This scent belongs in a horrendous dinner scene.

Use the tip list below as you create your scene.

- Sight: What does the scene look like? How are people placed at the table, what does the narrator notice about the food layout, the place settings, the decor, the people and their body language, the lighting, etc.? These details are vital for an unsuccessful meal.
- Smell: What aromas are filling the room? This could be from food, the room itself, the people at the table, etc.
- Sound: What sounds are there? Is there talking? What are the tones? Is no one talking and the only sound is clinking silverware?
- Touch: How does the tablecloth feel resting on the lap of your narrator? What about the napkins? The utensils? The chair?
- Taste: What do the drinks taste like? The food? Maybe the silverware leaves a lingering metallic taste?

EXERCISE 153

Objective: Write Flash Fiction

Task: Since circuses are so engaging and have helped shape the entertainment industry in America and around the world, study the 1920s advertisement (figure 2.2) titled, *Ringling Brothers and Barnum and Bailey Combined Shows*. The advertisement below shows children being amused by a clown while two other clowns watch from behind the circus tent curtains. Write a piece of flash fiction that is told either from the perspective of someone in this advertisement OR from a third-person narrator and be sure to describe the scene.

Flash Fiction is essentially a very short story that is usually under 500 words and tells a complete story. Be sure to include the setting, characterization, conflict or tension, and a resolution (no cliffhangers allowed).

Figure 2.2   (Exercise 153) Combined Shows Poster. *Source*: Billy Rose Theatre Division, The New York Public Library. The New York Public Library Digital Collections. 1920. https://digitalcollections.nypl.org/items/510d47da-4ed4-a3d9-e040-e00a18064a99.

EXERCISE 154

Objective: Enhance Sentences with Strategic Verb Choices and Tense Shifts

Task:

Step One: Read the sentence below.

> He got ready for work.

Step Two: What actions would need to take place to be ready for work? What verbs would be used? See the sample below for guidance:

Sample Sentence: She got ready to skate.
Sample verb list for skating: lacing/ tying/ stretching/ shining/ pinning/ layering

Step Three: Rewrite the original sentence using as many of the verbs from your list as you can. You can write as many sentences as you need to show readers that the character is ready for work.
   See the sample below as a reference:

Sample Revision: She pinned her stray hairs into place on top of her head, and then stretched her back in a large cat-like arch, stretching her arms by swinging them like windmills. She shined each blade with care before sliding her foot into the boot, lacing them up tightly. Her jacket layered onto her street clothes allowed her ample movement and kept her warm as she stood and waited for her turn to take the ice.

Step Four: Examine the exercise you just wrote. Which tense did you use? If you wrote in the past tense, rewrite the exercise in the present tense. If you wrote in the present tense, change it to the past tense. Which tense sounds best to you as you reread?

EXERCISE 155

Objective: Enhance Descriptive Writing by Selecting Specific Details

Task:

Step One: In one sentence, describe a chair.

Step Two: In one sentence, describe a person.

Step Three: Think of a specific chair that you know very well. Describe it in as much detail as you can. Use as many sentences as you need. Then reflect, is this the same chair that you described in sentence one? (It is okay if it isn't.)

Step Four: Associate a person with THAT specific chair that you just described in detail. Describe this person as specifically as you can. Use as many sentences as you need. Then reflect, Is this the same person that you described at the start of the exercise? How does this description differ?

Step Five: Write a paragraph where you include four of the five senses, the chair, and the person along with some action. Use your adjectives to target a specific tone. List the desired tone below. Sample tones might include calm, bold, comforting, comic, nostalgic, vibrant, tranquil, apprehensive, etc. _____

EXERCISE 156

Objective: Create Symbols

Task: Symbolism is a concept where a physical object represents some other concept. For example, a wedding ring symbolizes the never-ending circle of love in a marriage, or a dove represents peace and hope.

For example, windshield wipers could be a symbol for

- Wiping away emotions
- Changing moods
- A fresh slate
- Forgiveness
- Revealing truths

Step One: For this exercise, choose one of the concepts listed above and think of other objects that could symbolize that same concept. So, if you choose a fresh slate, what other everyday items might symbolize a fresh slate? List those items below:

_____

Step Two: Replace "windshield wipers" with another everyday item, and think of at least two bullets with potential symbolic meanings for that object.

Step Three: Write a 100–300 word scene on any subject and incorporate your everyday item in a symbolic way.

EXERCISE 157

Objective: Write Dynamically to Increase Audience Interest

Task: Imagine you were to turn a major point in your life into a movie or book. How would you convince people to watch or read it? What would your synopsis say?

Step One: Brainstorm your synopsis before you begin writing.

Consider:

1. Character (which is you): How do you want the audience to be introduced to you? What do you want to reveal to them? How can you communicate your motivations, fears, etc.?
2. Major conflict: What overarching conflict do you want to highlight in your synopsis? Is it a search for love? An interaction with a stranger that changed your life? A major life-changing crossroads you must navigate? What is it your character (you) wants?
3. Diction: What dynamic diction do you want to use?
4. Mood: What emotional components should you include?

Step Two: Write a synopsis including these components. It should be about 500 words and should convince your audience to watch or read your story.

EXERCISE 158

Objective: Write Poetry

Task: Write a poem titled "Facing Reality." Experiment with different elements to help your poem have a rich meaning. Use the poem planning notes below before you begin writing.

- Content: What is your poem about? Is it about facing reality in general and being more realistic than optimistic? Or is it more specific like facing a moment head-on when most people try to avoid it or cower from it?
- Tone: What is the overall tone you want to evoke? Are there other, supporting tones you want to use? Do you want to have your tone turn from optimistic to realistic? If so, your tone shifts can reinforce this transition. Consider how you can incorporate multiple tones to deliver your message.
- Punctuation: How can your punctuation help support the tone(s) you desire? For example, a hard tone can be evoked through short, direct sentences. Utilizing rhetorical questions, or even hypophora (when those questions are answered) can help deliver those tone(s) as well.
- Rhyme scheme: Your poem doesn't have to rhyme. But, if it does, how can you pair words or manipulate the rhythm of your poem to deliver your tone(s) and message?
- Language: What specific words can you use to develop your tone(s)? Also, what metaphors, similes, etc. can you use to develop that tone(s)?

Once you plan, begin writing!

EXERCISE 159

Objective: Practice with Characterization and Tone

Task: Create a dramatically emotional opening to a novel. The novel can be about anything. There are three rules.

- The first rule is that you must choose between a dismal tone or an exuberant one.
- The second rule is that you must plan and utilize the PAIRS acronym to create indirect characterization. Your main character should either be very young or very old and either very rich or very poor. The "P" stands for physical description, the "A" stands for action, the "I" stands for inner thoughts, the "R" stands for reactions, and the "S" stands for speech.
- The third rule is that you must start with dialogue.

Step One: Develop your character using the PAIRS acronym. Remember the second rule when planning.

P:

A:

I:

R:

S:

Step Two: Write your opening. Remember, characterization is meant to be shown and not told. Your opening scene should be about 400–500 words. You can start anywhere in the plot, but you must start with dialogue.

EXERCISE 160

Objective: Practice with Different Genres of Writing

(Note: Writers will need to complete a prose writing prompt from Section Three to complete this prompt.)

Task:

Step One: Reread your prose from any activity in Section Three.

Step Two: Rewrite your activity from Section Three turning your prose into verse.

When transforming your work to verse, here are some things to consider:

- Line length: You are going to want some lines to be longer than others.
- Shape: You need to consider what you want your poem to look like and how you can manipulate the shape of it to help deliver drama. For example, providing extra spacing between words to mimic hesitation or stress.
- Content: Not everything from your opening might fit into verse but you are going to want to include the most important details. Which details belong?
- Rhythm: Your poem does not have to rhyme. However, you will want to create a rhythm that reinforces the tone you want to evoke.
- Rich language: Because you don't have the same space for details as you do in prose, you will need to be creative with your language. You might want to think about which evocative literary devices you can include.

Section Three

45-Minute Exercises

EXERCISE 161

Objective: Eliminate Filler Words in Narrative Writing

Task:

Step One: Read the introduction of *The Murder of Roger Ackroyd* by Agatha Christie, published in 1926. This entire opening is written in first-person past tense, making it a memory. Read carefully and look to see if you find any "filler words" in this memory. Filler words include words such as really, very, that, even, just, in order to, and basically.

> Mrs. Ferrars died on the night of the 16th–17th September—a Thursday.
>
> I was sent for at eight o'clock on the morning of Friday the 17th. There was nothing to be done. She had been dead some hours.
>
> It was just a few minutes after nine when I reached home once more. I opened the front door with my latch-key, and purposely delayed a few moments in the hall, hanging up my hat and the light overcoat that I had deemed a wise precaution against the chill of an early autumn morning. To tell the truth, I was considerably upset and worried. I am not going to pretend that at that moment I foresaw the events of the next few weeks. I emphatically did not do so. But my instinct told me that there were stirring times ahead.
>
> From the dining-room on my left there came the rattle of tea-cups and the short, dry cough of my sister Caroline.
>
> "Is that you, James?" she called.
>
> An unnecessary question, since who else could it be? To tell the truth, it was precisely my sister Caroline who was the cause of my few minutes' delay. The motto of the mongoose family, so Mr. Kipling tells us, is: "Go and find out." If Caroline ever adopts a crest, I should certainly suggest a mongoose rampant. One might omit the first part of the motto. Caroline can do any amount of finding out by sitting placidly at home. I don't know how she manages it, but there it is. I suspect that the servants and the tradesmen constitute her Intelligence Corps. When she goes out, it is not to gather in information, but to spread it. At that, too, she is amazingly expert.
>
> It was really this last named trait of hers which was causing me these pangs of indecision. Whatever I told Caroline now concerning the demise of Mrs. Ferrars would be common knowledge all over the village within the space of an hour and a half. As a professional man, I naturally aim at discretion. Therefore I have got into the habit of continually withholding all information possible from my sister. She usually finds out just the same, but I have the moral satisfaction of knowing that I am in no way to blame.
>
> Mrs. Ferrars' husband died just over a year ago, and Caroline has constantly asserted, without the least foundation for the assertion, that his wife poisoned him.

Step Two: Circle or list every time Agatha Christie used the word "that" and then cross it out and read the sentence again. You will notice each sentence would be just fine without including "that."

Step Three: Spend twenty minutes writing about a memory of a person you live with (or once lived with).

Step Four: Look back over your work and circle ALL the filler words that were outlined in Step One. Revise your writing to eliminate these filler words.

EXERCISE 162

Objective: Evaluate Rhetoric and Practice Using Rhetoric in Argumentation

Task:

Step One: Evaluate Queen Elizabeth's speech to her troops delivered in 1588. Take a minute to consider the time period, her gender, and her sentiments and rhetoric.

While reading the speech, take notes on the following details:

- Diction—What strong word choice does she employ to convince her soldiers to follow her into battle?
- Pathos—What emotions does she evoke and how does she do it?
- Ethos—How does she convince the soldiers she's worthy of their loyalty?
- Structure—How does she start her speech? How does she end it? How does she use repetition to her advantage?

Queen Elizabeth I's Speech to the Troops at Tilbury, 1588

My loving people, We have been persuaded by some that are careful of our safety, to take heed how we commit ourselves to armed multitudes, for fear of treachery; but I assure you I do not desire to live to distrust my faithful and loving people. Let tyrants fear, I have always so behaved myself that, under God, I have placed my chiefest strength and safeguard in the loyal hearts and good-will of my subjects; and therefore I am come amongst you, as you see, at this time, not for my recreation and disport, but being resolved, in the midst and heat of the battle, to live and die amongst you all; to lay down for my God, and for my kingdom, and my people, my honour and my blood, even in the dust. I know I have the body but of a weak and feeble woman; but I have the heart and stomach of a king, and of a king of England too, and think foul scorn that Parma or Spain, or any prince of Europe, should dare to invade the borders of my realm; to which rather than any dishonour shall grow by me, I myself will take up arms, I myself will be your general, judge, and rewarder of every one of your virtues in the field. I know already, for your forwardness you have deserved rewards and crowns; and We do assure you in the word of a prince, they shall be duly paid you. In the meantime, my lieutenant general shall be in my stead, than whom never prince commanded a more noble or worthy subject; not doubting but by your obedience to my general, by your concord in the camp, and your valour in the field, we shall shortly have a famous victory over those enemies of my God, of my kingdom, and of my people.

Step Two: Consider the notes you took while analyzing her speech. Now, write your own speech modeling her techniques. Match your audience to her audience. It doesn't have to be as dire as going off to battle. Meaning, write your speech to a crowd who might discredit you. For example, it could be a panel of interviewers who think you might be underqualified for a job.

EXERCISE 163

Objective: Analyze Poetry for Important Literal and Figurative Meaning and Use that Analysis to Construct a Commemorative Poem

Task:

Step One: Read the poem "O Captain! My Captain!" by Walt Whitman, published in 1865. It's important to note that this poem was written to commemorate Abraham Lincoln after his assassination. Use this knowledge and perspective to interpret the poem.

> O Captain! my Captain! our fearful trip is done,
> The ship has weather'd every rack, the prize we sought is won,
> The port is near, the bells I hear, the people all exulting,
> While follow eyes the steady keel, the vessel grim and daring;
> > But O heart! heart! heart!
> > O the bleeding drops of red,
> > Where on the deck my Captain lies,
> > Fallen cold and dead.
>
> O Captain! my Captain! rise up and hear the bells;
> Rise up—for you the flag is flung—for you the bugle trills,
> For you bouquets and ribbon'd wreaths—for you the shores a-crowding,
> For you they call, the swaying mass, their eager faces turning;
> > Here Captain! dear father!
> > This arm beneath your head!
> > It is some dream that on the deck,
> > You've fallen cold and dead.
>
> My Captain does not answer, his lips are pale and still,
> My father does not feel my arm, he has no pulse nor will,
> The ship is anchor'd safe and sound, its voyage closed and done,
> From fearful trip the victor ship comes in with object won;
> > Exult O shores, and ring O bells!
> > But I with mournful tread,
> > Walk the deck my Captain lies,
> > Fallen cold and dead.

Step Two: Commemorative Poem Planning Guide

After reading and analyzing "O Captain! My Captain!", consider the following elements implemented throughout the poem so you can model your poem after Walt Whitman's. Use the planning guide below for guidance.

1. Conceit: Whitman incorporated an all-encompassing extended metaphor comparing Lincoln to a captain of a ship. This metaphor is unique, complex, and a bit surprising. That's what makes it so fantastic. What extended metaphor could you compare your person to?
2. Rhyme Scheme: Whitman utilizes an AABBCDED rhyme scheme. Consider modeling this rhyme scheme in your own poem.
3. Punctuation: Whitman employs a variety of punctuation to evoke tone throughout the poem. The use of exclamation points and dashes helps evoke his tone. Consider utilizing strategic punctuation to help deliver your desired tone.
4. Syntax: Whitman incorporates a variety of sentence structures. He contrasts long thoughts with short ones. This draws attention to both lines of poetry. Consider altering your line length to add emphasis to special details.
5. Apostrophe: Whitman is writing to an audience that is not there. Yet, it still has a reverent tone even though Lincoln will never read it. Evoke that same tone through apostrophe.
6. Repetition: Whitman, in several places, uses repetition. Not only does he repeat phrases within the same lines, but he starts several lines with the same opening phrase—which is called anaphora. He also ends each stanza with a repeated phrase—which is called epistrophe. Consider utilizing repetition strategically in your own poem.

Step Three: Create your own poem commemorating a different important figure. Use the planning from Step Two to guide you as you write.

EXERCISE 164

Objective: Create a Setting Incorporating Vivid Details and Clear Imagery

Task: The following excerpt is a description of a haunted room that appeared in Sir Edward Bulwer-Lytton's story, *The Haunted and the Haunters*, which was published in 1859.

Step One: Read the excerpt and circle or list 8–10 words that stand out to you as being particularly vivid.

> Before he had finished his sentence, the door, which neither of us then was touching, opened quietly of itself. We looked at each other a single instant. The same thought seized both—some human agency might be detected here. I rushed in first, my servant followed. A small blank dreary room without furniture—a few empty boxes and hampers in a corner—a small window—the shutters closed—not even a fireplace—no other door but that by which we had entered—no carpet on the food, and the floor seemed very old, uneven, worm-eaten, mended here and there, as was shown by the whiter patches on the wood; but no living being, and no visible place in which a living being could have hidden. As we stood gazing around, the door by which we had entered closed as quietly as it had before opened: we were imprisoned.

Step Two: What is the tone of this excerpt? _____

Notice that this excerpt opens and closes, quite literally, with the opening and closing of a door, creating nice bookends for the description in the middle. The description is laden with adjectives as well as en dashes, rather than commas, to separate the details.

Step Three: Use this text as a model to create your own description of a room—any room you wish. You can create any mood you wish, but you should:

1. Incorporate the 8–10 words that you circled or listed from the excerpt above.
2. Try to separate details about the room with en dashes rather than commas.
3. Begin your writing with some kind of action.
4. Create a specific tone that can be easily identified.

EXERCISE 165

Objective: Evaluate an Opening to a Novella and Then Create an Opening to a Different Novella Modeling What was Done Well and Changing What Could be Better

Task:

Step One: Evaluate the following opening to the novella *The Metamorphosis*, published in 1915. When you evaluate, consider some of the following criteria and whether you like how Franz Kafka did it:

- Conflict—How is the conflict of the novella introduced? Is it even introduced at all? Do you like this method?
- Characterization—How is the character introduced? Developed?
- Plot—Where does the plot line start?
- Entertainment—Is it exciting? Does it make you want to continue reading?

> One morning, when Gregor Samsa woke from troubled dreams, he found himself transformed in his bed into a horrible vermin. He lay on his armour-like back, and if he lifted his head a little he could see his brown belly, slightly domed and divided by arches into stiff sections. The bedding was hardly able to cover it and seemed ready to slide off any moment. His many legs, pitifully thin compared with the size of the rest of him, waved about helplessly as he looked.
> "What's happened to me?" he thought. It wasn't a dream. His room, a proper human room although a little too small, lay peacefully between its four familiar walls. A collection of textile samples lay spread out on the table—Samsa was a travelling salesman—and above it there hung a picture that he had recently cut out of an illustrated magazine and housed in a nice, gilded frame. It showed a lady fitted out with a fur hat and fur boa who sat upright, raising a heavy fur muff that covered the whole of her lower arm towards the viewer.
> Gregor then turned to look out the window at the dull weather. Drops of rain could be heard hitting the pane, which made him feel quite sad. "How about if I sleep a little bit longer and forget all this nonsense," he thought, but that was something he was unable to do because he was used to sleeping on his right, and in his present state couldn't get into that position. However hard he threw himself onto his right, he always rolled back to where he was. He must have tried it a hundred times, shut his eyes so that he wouldn't have to look at the floundering legs, and only stopped when he began to feel a mild, dull pain there that he had never felt before.
> "Oh, God," he thought, "what a strenuous career it is that I've chosen! Travelling day in and day out. Doing business like this takes much more effort than

doing your own business at home, and on top of that there's the curse of travelling, worries about making train connections, bad and irregular food, contact with different people all the time so that you can never get to know anyone or become friendly with them. It can all go to Hell!" He felt a slight itch up on his belly; pushed himself slowly up on his back towards the headboard so that he could lift his head better; found where the itch was, and saw that it was covered with lots of little white spots which he didn't know what to make of; and when he tried to feel the place with one of his legs he drew it quickly back because as soon as he touched it he was overcome by a cold shudder.

Step Two: Plan an opening to a completely different novella. Have your character suddenly transform into something completely different, as Kafka did with Gregor.

Consider your evaluation of Kafka's opening scene. Model what you think was done well and change what you think could have been done better.

Use the questions below to brainstorm your novella opening.

- Conflict—What is the conflict(s) in your novella? How do you want to introduce conflict in your opening?
- Characterization—Who is your character? How will he or she react to the transformation?
- Plot—Where and how does your plot line start? What is the transformation taking place and how do you plan on revealing it to your readers?
- Entertainment—How do you plan on making your opening exciting? What will you do to entice readers to keep reading?

Step Three: Once you have finished planning, begin writing.

Section Three

EXERCISE 166

Objective: Write an Epilogue while Incorporating Literary Elements

Task:

Step One: Read the following epilogue from *Alice's Adventures in Wonderland* by Lewis Carroll, published in 1865. You may already know that Alice chases a rabbit down a rabbit hole and that is where she discovers Wonderland and meets the Mad Hatter and the Queen of Hearts. The story ends with her waking from what seemed to be a "curious" dream. However, the novel truly ends with an epilogue from her sister's point of view.

Read the epilogue and analyze the following elements that typically go into epilogues:

- Pacing—How does this epilogue manipulate time or show time passing?
- Point of view—What does the switch in point of view add to the story?
- Information—What new information is brought to the story in the epilogue?
- Loose ends—How are loose ends tied up or left open for a sequel?

> But her sister sat still just as she left her, leaning her head on her hand, watching the setting sun, and thinking of little Alice and all her wonderful Adventures, till she too began dreaming after a fashion, and this was her dream:
>
> First, she dreamed of little Alice herself, and once again the tiny hands were clasped upon her knee, and the bright eager eyes were looking up into hers—she could hear the very tones of her voice, and see that queer little toss of her head to keep back the wandering hair that *would* always get into her eyes—and still as she listened, or seemed to listen, the whole place around her became alive with the strange creatures of her little sister's dream.
>
> The long grass rustled at her feet as the White Rabbit hurried by—the frightened Mouse splashed his way through the neighbouring pool—she could hear the rattle of the teacups as the March Hare and his friends shared their never-ending meal, and the shrill voice of the Queen ordering off her unfortunate guests to execution—once more the pig-baby was sneezing on the Duchess's knee, while plates and dishes crashed around it—once more the shriek of the Gryphon, the squeaking of the Lizard's slate-pencil, and the choking of the suppressed guinea-pigs, filled the air, mixed up with the distant sobs of the miserable Mock Turtle.
>
> So she sat on, with closed eyes, and half believed herself in Wonderland, though she knew she had but to open them again, and all would change to dull reality—the grass would be only rustling in the wind, and the pool rippling to the waving of the reeds—the rattling teacups would change to tinkling

sheep-bells, and the Queen's shrill cries to the voice of the shepherd boy—and the sneeze of the baby, the shriek of the Gryphon, and all the other queer noises, would change (she knew) to the confused clamour of the busy farm-yard—while the lowing of the cattle in the distance would take the place of the Mock Turtle's heavy sobs.

Lastly, she pictured to herself how this same little sister of hers would, in the after-time, be herself a grown woman; and how she would keep, through all her riper years, the simple and loving heart of her childhood: and how she would gather about her other little children, and make *their* eyes bright and eager with many a strange tale, perhaps even with the dream of Wonderland of long ago: and how she would feel with all their simple sorrows, and find a pleasure in all their simple joys, remembering her own child-life, and the happy summer days.

Step Two: Using your analysis from Step One, create your own epilogue to your favorite book or movie. Be sure to include:

- Pacing—send it into the future
- Point of view—provide a unique perspective
- New information—include details about the characters and where they end up
- Loose ends—tie up any loose ends

EXERCISE 167

Objective: Write a Scene with Rich Action

Task: In the following scene from Bram Stoker's *Dracula*, published in 1897, Renfield, a patient at the insane asylum near Dracula's domain, escapes and fights to be near Dracula.

Step One: Analyze this action scene and notice the sequence of events.

> Later.—Another night adventure. Renfield artfully waited until the attendant was entering the room to inspect. Then he dashed out past him and flew down the passage. I sent word for the attendants to follow. Again he went into the grounds of the deserted house, and we found him in the same place, pressed against the old chapel door. When he saw me he became furious, and had not the attendants seized him in time, he would have tried to kill me. As we were holding him a strange thing happened. He suddenly redoubled his efforts, and then as suddenly grew calm. I looked round instinctively, but could see nothing. Then I caught the patient's eye and followed it, but could trace nothing as it looked into the moonlight sky, except a big bat, which was flapping its silent and ghostly way to the west. Bats usually wheel about, but this one seemed to go straight on, as if it knew where it was bound for or had some intention of its own.
>
> The patient grew calmer every instant, and presently said, "You needn't tie me. I shall go quietly!" Without trouble, we came back to the house.

Step Two: Compare the sequence of events below to the excerpt:

1. Character craftily escapes from their entrapment
2. Character is pursued
3. Character goes to a desired second location
4. Character is angered at being caught
5. Character receives a secret message from an ally and immediately calms
6. Character agrees to enter back into their original entrapment

This list of events is nowhere near as exciting to read as the original account written by Bram Stoker. Notice the details Stoker incorporates that make this excerpt thrilling to read. Pay attention to the verbs, the adjectives, the way the action is portrayed, and the insertion of the narrator's thoughts—all of this enhances the narrative.

Step Three: Create an action scene that has different characters and different settings, but that follows a similar plot sequence to the one outlined in Step Two.

EXERCISE 168

Objective: Use Poetry to Stem Narrative Fiction While Practicing With Imagery

Task:

Step One: Read and analyze the poem *Dulce Et Decorum Est*, by Wilfred Owen, published in 1920. Be sure to analyze the sentiments, tone, and imagery within the poem. When analyzing imagery, be sure to notice visual and auditory imagery.

> Bent double, like old beggars under sacks,
> Knock-kneed, coughing like hags, we cursed through sludge,
> Till on the haunting flares we turned our backs,
> And towards our distant rest began to trudge.
> Men marched asleep. Many had lost their boots,
> But limped on, blood-shod. All went lame; all blind;
> Drunk with fatigue; deaf even to the hoots
> Of gas-shells dropping softly behind.
>
> Gas! GAS! Quick, boys!—An ecstasy of fumbling
> Fitting the clumsy helmets just in time,
> But someone still was yelling out and stumbling
> And flound'ring like a man in fire or lime.—
> Dim through the misty panes and thick green light,
> As under a green sea, I saw him drowning.
> In all my dreams before my helpless sight,
> He plunges at me, guttering, choking, drowning.
>
> If in some smothering dreams, you too could pace
> Behind the wagon that we flung him in,
> And watch the white eyes writhing in his face,
> His hanging face, like a devil's sick of sin;
> If you could hear, at every jolt, the blood
> Come gargling from the froth-corrupted lungs,
> Obscene as cancer, bitter as the cud
> Of vile, incurable sores on innocent tongues,—
> My friend, you would not tell with such high zest
> To children ardent for some desperate glory,
> The old Lie: *Dulce et decorum est
> Pro patria mori.*

Step Two: Choose one of the stanzas to turn into a scene that would belong in a novel. You might want to include dialogue, setting, more in-depth plot points, etc.

In your scene, be sure to include:

- Visual imagery
- Auditory imagery
- Similar tones
- Indirect characterization: Be sure to show your readers the motivations, emotions, etc. without directly telling them. Leave them to infer based on your carefully crafted details.

EXERCISE 169

Objective: Analyze the Effectiveness of Dialogue and Showing vs. Telling

Task:

Step One: Read the sample dialogue below, where a brother reveals that he has been stealing money from his older sister. Circle or list the areas where you sense heightened emotions. What emotions stand out the most? How were they developed?

> "Did you steal from me? Be honest, Hunter. I have to know." Amber asked, barely containing her anger.
> "Yes, but only when I absolutely needed it. I never stole for anything that wasn't important. I promise." Hunter said.
> "You can't expect me to believe you after this!" she yelled.
> "But it was really important!"

Step Two: Read the sample of prose below where the sister finds her brother stealing from her. Pay attention to the emotion in the scene. Circle or list the areas where you sense heightened emotions. What emotions stand out the most? How were they developed?

> Keys still in the door, I paused, listening as someone shuffled papers on my desk and opened drawers under my keyboard. My hand shook in its place, frozen on the door handle when the rustling in the next room stopped and I presumed we were both standing still, listening for one another. My own heart hammered so loudly I was convinced the entire apartment building could hear it, but I couldn't bring myself to move, back up, close the door, or run. My brain told my legs to move it, to get out of there, but my legs decided that staying put, like a deer in the crosshairs, was a better move.
> Soft steps padded across the carpet towards me, and I slowly removed my hand from the door handle, trying not to jostle the keys as Hunter made his way into the living room, stuffing something in his pocket just as he turned the corner.
> "Hunter?" I asked. "What are you doing here?"
> He looked instinctively back towards my bedroom then focused his attention on me fully. "Just looking for my social security card."
> "In *my* desk?"
> "Uh. Yeah."
> "Hunter, show me what is in your pocket."

Hunter looked to the ground as he pulled out the envelope of cash I had been saving for vacation this summer. "But it was important!" he all but shouted as he saw my face darken.

Step Three: Now, craft a scenario and write the scene once using just dialogue that is TELLING what is happening, similar to the sample from Step One.

Step Four: Write the scene once more using action that is SHOWING what is happening, similar to the sample from Step Two, and see which you like best.

EXERCISE 170

Objective: Redesign a Classic Scene for a Young Adult or Middle-Grade Audience

Task:

Step One: Read and analyze the scene from *Dr. Jekyll and Mr. Hyde*, written by Robert Louis Stevenson and published in 1886. In this scene, Henry Jekyll reflects on the discovery of Hyde (his dangerous alter ego). When analyzing, be sure to explore how Jekyll feels about the presence of Hyde and the characterization of both characters and their significance.

> The most racking pangs succeeded: a grinding in the bones, deadly nausea, and a horror of the spirit that cannot be exceeded at the hour of birth or death. Then these agonies began swiftly to subside, and I came to myself as if out of a great sickness. There was something strange in my sensations, something indescribably new and, from its very novelty, incredibly sweet. I felt younger, lighter, happier in body; within I was conscious of a heady recklessness, a current of disordered sensual images running like a millrace in my fancy, a solution of the bonds of obligation, an unknown but not an innocent freedom of the soul. I knew myself, at the first breath of this new life, to be more wicked, tenfold more wicked, sold a slave to my original evil; and the thought, in that moment, braced and delighted me like wine. I stretched out my hands, exulting in the freshness of these sensations; and in the act, I was suddenly aware that I had lost in stature.
>
> There was no mirror, at that date, in my room; that which stands beside me as I write, was brought there later on and for the very purpose of these transformations. The night however, was far gone into the morning—the morning, black as it was, was nearly ripe for the conception of the day—the inmates of my house were locked in the most rigorous hours of slumber; and I determined, flushed as I was with hope and triumph, to venture in my new shape as far as to my bedroom. I crossed the yard, wherein the constellations looked down upon me, I could have thought, with wonder, the first creature of that sort that their unsleeping vigilance had yet disclosed to them; I stole through the corridors, a stranger in my own house; and coming to my room, I saw for the first time the appearance of Edward Hyde.
>
> I must here speak by theory alone, saying not that which I know, but that which I suppose to be most probable. The evil side of my nature, to which I had now transferred the stamping efficacy, was less robust and less developed than the good which I had just deposed. Again, in the course of my life, which had been, after all, nine tenths a life of effort, virtue and control, it had been much less exercised and much less exhausted. And hence, as I think, it came about that Edward Hyde was so much smaller, slighter and younger than Henry Jekyll. Even as good shone upon the countenance of the one, evil was

written broadly and plainly on the face of the other. Evil besides (which I must still believe to be the lethal side of man) had left on that body an imprint of deformity and decay. And yet when I looked upon that ugly idol in the glass, I was conscious of no repugnance, rather of a leap of welcome. This, too, was myself. It seemed natural and human. In my eyes it bore a livelier image of the spirit, it seemed more express and single, than the imperfect and divided countenance I had been hitherto accustomed to call mine. And in so far I was doubtless right. I have observed that when I wore the semblance of Edward Hyde, none could come near to me at first without a visible misgiving of the flesh. This, as I take it, was because all human beings, as we meet them, are commingled out of good and evil: and Edward Hyde, alone in the ranks of mankind, was pure evil.

Step Two: Redesign this scene. Your audience is contemporary and either middle-grade or young adult readers. Create a contemporary and age-appropriate Jekyll and Hyde. The details of your story can be different, but the characterization and emotions Jekyll feels towards Hyde should be the same.

EXERCISE 171

Objective: Write a Fictional Scene from Two Sources

Task:

Step One: Read this love poem published in 1599 by Christopher Marlowe titled, "The Passionate Shepherd to His Love," and compare it to the etching (figure 3.1) by Francesco Londonio titled, *Seated Old Man and Woman with a Basket of Eggs, 1759/1782.*

>Come live with me and be my love,
>And we will all the pleasures prove,
>That Valleys, groves, hills, and fields,
>Woods, or steepy mountain yields.
>
>And we will sit upon the Rocks,
>Seeing the Shepherds feed their flocks,
>By shallow Rivers to whose falls
>Melodious birds sing Madrigals.
>
>And I will make thee beds of Roses
>And a thousand fragrant posies,
>A cap of flowers, and a kirtle
>Embroidered all with leaves of Myrtle;
>
>A gown made of the finest wool
>Which from our pretty Lambs we pull;
>Fair lined slippers for the cold,
>With buckles of the purest gold;
>
>A belt of straw and Ivy buds,
>With Coral clasps and Amber studs:
>And if these pleasures may thee move,
>Come live with me, and be my love.
>
>The Shepherds' Swains shall dance and sing
>For thy delight each May-morning:
>If these delights thy mind may move,
>Then live with me, and be my love.

Figure 3.1 (Exercise 171) Woman with Basket. *Source*: Etching by Francesco Londonio titled, *Seated Old Man and Woman with a Basket of Eggs*, 1759/1782.

Step Two: List the differences in the way the life of a shepherd's wife is depicted in the poem vs. the etching.

Step Three: Write a scene in which the shepherd's love from the poem either denies his proposal and breaks his heart or accepts his proposal and joins him in his shepherding life. Ensure items from your list from Step Two make their way into the scene.

45-Minute Exercises 131

EXERCISE 172

Objective: Use Historical Documents to Stem Fiction

Task: Use the newspaper headlines to write a diary entry from someone on December 31, 1922.

Step One: Examine the newspaper headlines (figure 3.2) from *The Bridgepoint Times* on the 31st of December 1922. While you examine the headlines, make five notes about what you think life was like during this time period.

Figure 3.2 (Exercise 172) The Bridgeport Times. *Source*: The people's voice. [volume] (Helena, Mont.), 31 Oct. 1952. Chronicling America: Historic American Newspapers. Lib. of Congress. <https://chroniclingamerica.loc.gov/lccn/sn86075189/1952-10-31/ed-1/seq-5/>

Step Two: Plan your journal entry. As you plan, remember to incorporate your five notes about what life was like.

Perspective:

- Whose voice do you want to capture in your journal?
- Who is your character?
- How old is your character?
- What is the economic situation of your character?

Details from the newspaper:

- Which specific element do you want to highlight?
- What emotion should you try to capture?

Plot:

- What happened on the day you're writing about (specific to your character)?
- What moment do you want to capture?
- What do you want to highlight to readers?

Step Three: Write your journal entry. When writing your journal entry, try to make the voice match your perspective, your details depict the reality of the era, and the conflict capture your readers. Make sure elements from your planning make it into your journal entry.

EXERCISE 173

Objective: Analyze and Recreate an Argument

Task:

Step One: Read the opening of the third chapter of *Winnie-The-Pooh*, written by A. A. Milne and published in 1926. Pay special attention to the argument Piglet is making about the sign outside his house and his grandfather's name. Identify Piglet's flawed logic.

> The Piglet lived in a very grand house in the middle of a beech-tree, and the beech-tree was in the middle of the forest, and the Piglet lived in the middle of the house. Next to his house was a piece of broken board which had: "TRESPASSERS W" on it. When Christopher Robin asked the Piglet what it meant, he said it was his grandfather's name, and had been in the family for a long time, Christopher Robin said you couldn't be called Trespassers W, and Piglet said yes, you could, because his grandfather was, and it was short for Trespassers Will, which was short for Trespassers William. And his grandfather had had two names in case he lost one—Trespassers after an uncle, and William after Trespassers.
>
> "I've got two names," said Christopher Robin carelessly.
>
> "Well, there you are, that proves it," said Piglet.

Step Two: Then look at the picture (figure 3.3) with the broken sign and speculate what the sign may have once said.

Figure 3.3 (Exercise 173) Winnie the Pooh. *Source*: Milne, A A, Shepard, Ernest, Winnie the Pooh, Canada: McClelland & Stewart, Ltd.,1926, pubdate 1926, pubdate 1931.

Step Three: Using that argument as a template, create an illogical argument between two characters where one character is CLEARLY jumping to the wrong conclusion, and yet backing themselves up with what they *think* is appropriate evidence.

EXERCISE 174

Objective: Use Poetry to Stem Narrative Fiction and Practice with Indirect Characterization

Task:

Step One: Read the poem "The Forsaken Wife" by Elizabeth Thomas, written in 1722. Identify the sentiments, tone, and characterization within the poem. Make notes while reading that highlight who the narrator is, how she feels, what motivates her, how her tone changes, and how she feels about her marriage.

> Methinks, 'tis strange you can't afford
> One pitying look, one parting word;
> Humanity claims this as due,
> But what's humanity to you?
>
> Cruel man! I am not blind,
> Your infidelity I find;
> Your want of love my ruin shows,
> My broken heart, your broken vows.
>
> Yet maugre all your rigid hate,
> I will be true in spite of fate;
> And one preeminence I'll claim,
> To be for ever still the same.
>
> Show me a man that dare be true,
> That dares to suffer what I do;
> That can for ever sigh unheard,
> And ever love without regard:
> I then will own your prior claim
> To love, to honour, and to fame;
> But till that time, my dear, adieu,
> I yet superior am to you.

Step Two: Plan a short story. You are either

Option One: Continuing the sentiments within the poem for our narrator or
Option Two: Describing the incidences or moments leading up to this moment.

Use the space provided to brainstorm ideas for each option.

Option One   Option Two

You should keep the same point of view as the poem and include:

- Indirect characterization: Be sure to show your readers her motivations, emotions, etc. without directly telling them. Leave them to infer based on your carefully crafted details.
- Tone(s): Consider the tone(s) you identified within the poem. Don't forget them when you write your prose.

Step Three: Choose which route you want to take (Option One or Two) and write your short story.

A reminder:

- Make sure you aren't just retelling the poem. The story is outside the poem. You are either writing about the aftermath once the poem was written or you are detailing the moments leading up to the writing of the poem.

EXERCISE 175

Objective: Write a Fictional Scene from Two Sources

Task: Numerous poems and pieces of art depict the enchantments of the night and the splendor of the moon. Two samples are below: one, an albumen print (figure 3.4) by Eadweard Muybridge titled, *Moonlight Effect-Bay of Panama, 1877* and the other, a poem, "Meeting at Night" by Robert Browning published in 1845.

Step One: Study the print. Take note of the tone that is being depicted.

Figure 3.4 (Exercise 175) Moonlight. *Source*: Albumen print by Eadweard Muybridge titled, Moonlight Effect-Bay of Panama, 1877.

Step Two: As you read the poem, circle or list all the words in the poem that match the tone of the painting.

> The grey sea and the long black land;
> And the yellow half-moon large and low;
> And the startled little waves that leap
> In fiery ringlets from their sleep,
> As I gain the cove with pushing prow,
> And quench its speed i' the slushy sand.
>
> Then a mile of warm sea-scented beach;
> Three fields to cross till a farm appears;

> A tap at the pane, the quick sharp scratch
> And blue spurt of a lighted match,
> And a voice less loud, thro' its joys and fears,
> Than the two hearts beating each to each!

Step Three: Use the poem and the print as inspiration. Write a scene where two characters meet unexpectedly one night on a boardwalk overlooking the ocean. Try to incorporate as many of the words you circled or listed from the poem as possible as you try to match the tones.

EXERCISE 176

Objective: Determine Purpose and Use Textual Evidence to Write Argumentatively

Task:

Step One: After Japan bombed Pearl Harbor on December 7, 1941, the following day President Franklin Roosevelt addressed the nation and prepared them for war.

However, he was not the first to address the nation. His wife, First Lady Eleanor Roosevelt, was one of the first to officially speak about the bombing in a public manner and did so on her radio station where she was speaking to the women of the nation. The speech is titled *Pearl Harbor Attack Radio Address* and was delivered on December 7, 1941.

As you read, analyze her motivation and message. Be sure to analyze her diction, tone, punctuation, etc.

> Good evening, ladies and gentlemen, I am speaking to you tonight at a very serious moment in our history. The Cabinet is convening and the leaders in Congress are meeting with the President. The State Department and Army and Navy officials have been with the President all afternoon. In fact, the Japanese ambassador was talking to the president at the very time that Japan's airships were bombing our citizens in Hawaii and the Philippines and sinking one of our transports loaded with lumber on its way to Hawaii.
> By tomorrow morning the members of Congress will have a full report and be ready for action.
> In the meantime, we the people are already prepared for action. For months now the knowledge that something of this kind might happen has been hanging over our heads and yet it seemed impossible to believe, impossible to drop the everyday things of life and feel that there was only one thing which was important—preparation to meet an enemy no matter where he struck. That is all over now and there is no more uncertainty.
> We know what we have to face and we know that we are ready to face it.

Step Two: Write a scene of a family listening to this speech. Recreate this moment through plot, dialogue, imagery, etc. This scene needs to look like it was plucked out of a novel, do not just summarize what the family might have been doing. Show- don't tell.

A few things to remember,

- They would have been listening to the speech on a radio, not watching it on a television.
- The bombing of Pearl Harbor happened around 8:00 a.m.
- Many members of the audience would have been females, mainly mothers. Their sons, like the president's, might have been in the military.
- Houses were mostly modest because the emphasis was on kids playing outside.
- Many wives and mothers were stay-at-home moms.
- Her show typically aired in the early afternoons.

EXERCISE 177

Objective: Write Scenes Based on Poetry

Task:

Step One: Read the following poem published by Thomas Hardy in 1914 titled, "*A Thunderstorm in Town.*"

> She wore a new 'terra-cotta' dress,
> And we stayed, because of the pelting storm,
> Within the hansom's dry recess,
> Though the horse had stopped; yea, motionless
> We sat on, snug and warm.
>
> Then the downpour ceased, to my sharp sad pain,
> And the glass that had screened our forms before
> Flew up, and out she sprang to her door:
> I should have kissed her if the rain
> Had lasted a minute more.

Step Two: You are going to be asked to rewrite this poem in prose. Before you do that, plan your response using the following questions:

- Who is the woman in this poem?
- How old is she?
- What does she look like?
- What makes her laugh?
- What makes her upset?
- Who is the man in this poem?
- How old is he?
- What does he look like?
- What does he expect from life?
- What does he value?
- What holds him back?

Step Three: Take the scene that is depicted and write it in prose rather than in verse. As you write, really dive into the characteristics of each character. Explore the circumstances and the emotions that are being expressed, especially those of the narrator at the end of the poem. How is he feeling as he realized he missed his moment with her? Try to make the characters real in the recreated scene you write.

EXERCISE 178

Objective: Practice with Setting and Imagery

Task:

Step One: Consider the following picture (figure 3.5) titled *Old House in Newmarket, Maryland,* taken by Jack Delano in the 1940s.

As you examine the picture, write what the various spaces in the house might look, smell, sound, and feel like. Try to be as specific as possible. Do this twice. Consider the senses as if you are in the house in the 1940s and then again as if you are examining the house today. List multiple details for each sense. Be sure to write down your ideas. For example, in the 1940s, you might smell baking bread, but today, you might smell mold.

The 1940s:	Today:
Sight:	Sight:
Sound:	Sound:
Touch:	Touch:
Smell:	Smell:

Figure 3.5 (Exercise 178) Old House. *Source*: https://www.loc.gov/resource/fsa .8c02405/ Old house in Newmarket, Maryland.

Step Two: Using your notes from Step One, create a scene using this house as the main setting. You need to decide if you want your scene to be set in the 1940s or today. Be sure to incorporate the sensory details you outlined in Step One.

You can either create a premise of your own or use one of the following scenarios provided.

Scenarios:

1. A police officer searches the house because it was a major crime scene.
2. A young family bought this home thinking it would be the house of their dreams.

144   Section Three

EXERCISE 179

Objective: Create Scenes Based on Source Material

Task:

Step One: Read the opening of Chapter Two of *A Room with a View* by E. M. Forster published in 1908. As you read, circle or list every noun and underline or list every adjective. The first line has been done for you.

> It was pleasant to wake up in Florence, to open the eyes upon a bright bare room with a floor of red tiles which look clean though they are not; with a painted ceiling whereon pink griffins and blue amorini sport in a forest of yellow violins and bassoons. It was pleasant, too, to fling wide the windows, pinching the fingers in unfamiliar fastenings, to lean out into sunshine with beautiful hills and trees and marble churches opposite, and close below, the Arno, gurgling against the embankment of the road.
>
> Over the river men were at work with spades and sieves on the sandy foreshore, and on the river was a boat, also diligently employed for some mysterious end. An electric tram came rushing underneath the window. No one was inside it, except one tourist; but its platforms were overflowing with Italians, who preferred to stand. Children tried to hang on behind, and the conductor, with no malice, spat in their faces to make them let go. Then soldiers appeared—good-looking, undersized men—wearing each a knapsack covered with mangy fur, and a great-coat which had been cut for some larger soldier. Beside them walked officers, looking foolish and fierce, and before them went little boys, turning somersaults in time with the band. The tramcar became entangled in their ranks, and moved on painfully, like a caterpillar in a swarm of ants. One of the little boys fell down, and some white bullocks came out of an archway. Indeed, if it had not been for the good advice of an old man who was selling button-hooks, the road might never have got clear.

Step Two: After you read, circle, and underline, write an entirely new scene using as many of the nouns as possible in any order you wish. Try to incorporate some of the adjectives as well. The goal isn't to recreate this scene, but to use these nouns and adjectives as jumping-off points for your writing.

EXERCISE 180

Objective: Create Characters Based on Tone

Task:

Step One: Read this scene from the opening chapter of *Treasure Island* by Robert Louis Stevenson, published in 1882. As you read, circle or list elements of the narrative where Stevenson creates a menacing tone.

> How that personage haunted my dreams, I need scarcely tell you. On stormy nights, when the wind shook the four corners of the house and the surf roared along the cove and up the cliffs, I would see him in a thousand forms, and with a thousand diabolical expressions. Now the leg would be cut off at the knee, now at the hip; now he was a monstrous kind of a creature who had never had but the one leg, and that in the middle of his body. To see him leap and run and pursue me over hedge and ditch was the worst of nightmares. And altogether I paid pretty dear for my monthly fourpenny piece, in the shape of these abominable fancies.
>
> But though I was so terrified by the idea of the seafaring man with one leg, I was far less afraid of the captain himself than anybody else who knew him. There were nights when he took a deal more rum and water than his head would carry; and then he would sometimes sit and sing his wicked, old, wild sea-songs, minding nobody; but sometimes he would call for glasses round and force all the trembling company to listen to his stories or bear a chorus to his singing. Often I have heard the house shaking with "Yo-ho-ho, and a bottle of rum," all the neighbours joining in for dear life, with the fear of death upon them, and each singing louder than the other to avoid remark. For in these fits he was the most overriding companion ever known; he would slap his hand on the table for silence all round; he would fly up in a passion of anger at a question, or sometimes because none was put, and so he judged the company was not following his story. Nor would he allow anyone to leave the inn till he had drunk himself sleepy and reeled off to bed.
>
> His stories were what frightened people worst of all. Dreadful stories they were—about hanging, and walking the plank, and storms at sea, and the Dry Tortugas, and wild deeds and places on the Spanish Main. By his own account he must have lived his life among some of the wickedest men that God ever allowed upon the sea, and the language in which he told these stories shocked our plain country people almost as much as the crimes that he described. My father was always saying the inn would be ruined, for people would soon cease coming there to be tyrannized over and put down, and sent shivering to their beds; but I really believe his presence did us good. People were frightened at the time, but on looking back they rather liked it; it was a fine excitement in a quiet country life, and there was even a party of the younger men who pretended

to admire him, calling him a "true sea-dog" and a "real old salt" and such like names, and saying there was the sort of man that made England terrible at sea.

Step Two: Using a similarly menacing tone, write about someone, fictional or real, who is intimidating. Be sure to include specific examples that reveal details about the character, whether through dialogue or description.

About the Authors

MICHELLE LINDSEY BIOGRAPHY

Michelle Lindsey's award-winning teaching experience has a wide range. She teaches a variety of grades from 9 to 12 and from classes ranging from remedial English to AICE (Advanced International Certificate of Education) Cambridge courses, AP Seminar, AP Research, AP Literature, and Creative Writing with some Debate and Speech sprinkled into the mix. She blends her love of writing, knowledge from her MFA in Writing, and passion for learning into a classroom environment where students and writers thrive.

Michelle has various publications ranging from flash fiction to essays in a variety of mediums, including journals, academic journals, and online educational websites. She also co-authored *3 Minute Tips for Teachers: A Toolbox of Ideas for Teachers to Use for the Entire School Year* with her sister, Heather Garcia. When Michelle isn't in her classroom, she is either conducting online workshops internationally for teachers, showing them how to incorporate writing into their classrooms to increase student engagement and skills or conducting online workshops for students showing them how to find their voice and write with conviction. She has also hosted in-person workshops for students and teachers nationally and is available for bookings.

When Michelle isn't working with teachers or students, she hibernates in her Florida home hiding from the unbearable sun working on her massive *to-be-read* pile that has consumed her home office and bank account.

HEATHER GARCIA BIOGRAPHY

Heather Garcia has a BA in English, an MA in English, and an MFA in Writing. She hosts online writing workshops for students from across the world and writes for both online and print publications. She is also the co-author of the book *3-Minute Tips for Teachers: A Toolbox of Ideas for Teachers to Use for the Entire School Year* with her sister, Michelle Lindsey.

Heather Garcia has taught writing to high schoolers ranging from students needing remediation to students in Advanced Placement English courses. She is also a college professor, sharing her love for the craft of writing with incoming freshmen and sophomores.

Her current teaching assignment has extended to her coaching and mentoring middle and high school teachers from across her school district as an English Curriculum and Instruction Specialist. She hosts professional development opportunities intended to help teachers offer engaging writing and reading activities to their own students.

In her spare time, Heather reads incessantly, throws pottery on the pottery wheel (and has far too many hand-made bowls and flower pots all over her house), and spends time with her two children and husband as they distract her (in the best ways) from her writing.

www.ingramcontent.com/pod-product-compliance
Lightning Source LLC
Chambersburg PA
CBHW020741230426
43665CB00009B/508